THE LIFE
— *of a* —
DEAD MAN

THE LIFE
— of a —
DEAD MAN

CALEB PIERCE

Copyright © 2021 The Life Of A Dead Man By Caleb Pierce

All rights reserved. No part of this publication may be reproduced, stored in a retrieval system, or transmitted in any form or by any means—electronic, mechanical, photocopy, or any other—except for brief quotations in printed reviews, without permission in writing from the publisher and/or author.

Unless otherwise noted, all scripture references are from the New King James Version. Copyright © 1982 by Thomas Nelson, Inc. Used by permission. All rights reserved.

Scripture quotations marked NLT are taken from the Holy Bible, New Living Translation, copyright © 1996, 2004. Used by permission of Tyndale House Publishers, Inc., Carol Stream, Illinois 60188. All rights reserved.

Scripture quotations taken from the Amplified® Bible (AMPC), Copyright © 1954, 1958, 1962, 1964, 1965, 1987 by The Lockman Foundation. Used by permission. www.lockman.org

Published by:

The Lift Publishing Group | Website: TheLiftChurch.tv

Publish To Print | Website: PublishToPrint.org

Cover: Istockphoto.com | Stock photo ID 173542839

Author: Caleb Pierce

Website: CalebPierce.org

Contact: info@calebpierce.org

Special Market Sales:
Organizations, churches, pastors, and small group leaders can receive special discounts when purchasing this book and other resources from The Lift Church. For information, please call 865-773-0488 or visit us at TheLiftChurch.tv.

I dedicate this book to my precious wife, Ali. You love Jesus with unreserved passion and it shows in all that you do. I could never fully express how grateful I am to walk this journey with you!

CONTENTS

1 COME BOTHER ME — **10**
2 THAT'S NOT MY NAME — **18**
3 RAISING WOLVES — **28**
4 CONNECTION CONUNDRUMS — **36**
5 WIND & FIRE — **44**
6 DANGERS OF THE DARK — **54**
7 THE IMPOSTER'S INFAMY — **64**
8 THE ART OF ADAPTATION — **74**
9 OUTPOURINGS & ORANGE JUICE — **82**
10 THE WORTH OF WINTER — **90**
11 THE STORY DOESN'T END HERE — **100**
12 REVEALING THEN REVIVAL — **110**
13 KEEP SOWING — **120**
14 UNITED FORCE — **130**
15 STAY THE COURSE — **138**
16 A FAMILY FEUD — **148**
17 DESTINY DISTRACTIONS — **156**
18 RUDE AWAKENING — **164**

CHAPTER 1
COME BOTHER ME

What if you get to the end of your life and suddenly realize that you got it all wrong? What if you discover that you lived for everything except the one and only thing worth dying for? What if you come to understand that every breath you invested into the life you are now leaving behind was nothing more than water in a bucket full of holes? I fear that if most of us in the American Church were to step back and honestly audit our lives in light of eternity, we would quickly realize that we are not living the life God had in mind when He created us.

To some degree, I think we all know what it is like to live on the hamster wheel of dissatisfaction—always striving to fill the void gnawing deep within our soul. It is a ruthless cycle that seeks to endlessly imprison all who fall into her trap. Her whisper seductively promises that fulfillment is just on the other side of that which is out of our reach. That is why her words are so enticing. It's like the classic casino slot machine that gives the false impression that you could win the grand prize if you will try just one more time. Yet, after trying a thousand times to no avail, like a broken record, she'll still be singing, "just one more try."

Spoiler alert . . . following her voice will never bring true fulfillment. Though her argument be persuasive and compelling, it is never ending. Pursuing her empty promises of comfort and convenience will always leave you dry and empty. If you spend your life buying into that whisper, you will undoubtedly one day reach the end of your race and realize you spent all of your days running in the wrong direction.

Here is the truth of the matter. The reason so many in the Church are living such unfulfilled lives is because they have settled for a cheap counterfeit. They aren't living the life God created them to live. Until we die to the desire to live a life of our own making, we will stay on the hamster wheel, always running yet never gaining any ground.

The eyes of the Lord are searching the earth, looking for those willing to give their all; those who will exchange their dreams and desires for the call of Heaven. God is looking for men and women who are bold enough to die to self so that He may employ them in His master plan for this hour.

THE KINGDOM CRITERIA

The criteria for this Kingdom call is really quite simple. God is not reviewing your resume to see if you qualify. He is not making a pros and cons list comparing and contrasting your strengths and weaknesses. He is not concerned with what you bring to the table. For this mission, He is really just looking at one thing—are you dead?

I know this sounds strange but stay with me. Think about the Apostle Paul. How was God able to take a man who was viciously pursuing the destruction of the

Church and transform him into the premier leader of the very movement he was trying to destroy? In writing to the church of Galatia, Paul shared the secret to this mystery when he said, *"I have been crucified with Christ; it is no longer I who live, but Christ lives in me; and the life which I now live in the flesh I live by faith in the Son of God, who loved me and gave Himself for me." (Galatians 2:20)*

Paul was a dead man. He allowed God to bring him to the end of himself. For too long we've wanted to add God to our comfortable, self-made lives as a supplement. We want enough of Him to get us into Heaven but not so much of Him that He begins to interfere with our manmade utopia. We can never really live the life God has created for us to live until we die to the life we have fought so ruthlessly to establish.

WE CAN NEVER REALLY LIVE THE LIFE GOD HAS CREATED FOR US TO LIVE UNTIL WE DIE TO THE LIFE WE HAVE FOUGHT SO RUTHLESSLY TO ESTABLISH.

BOTHER ME AGAIN

About eight months after my son Judah was born I was scheduled to minister out of town for a week at a friend's church. I'm always honored when given the opportunity to pour into a congregation and hold up the arms of a local pastor. However, as a new dad, this was going to be my first trip away from my boy. While excited to minister, I was dreading leaving my son behind for a whole week. I was really torn! Thankfully, a few days before the event we were able to rearrange some things in my wife's schedule, so that she and Judah could come along.

We ended up having a tremendous meeting. God moved powerfully! But I must confess that I was a bit shortsighted. Let me explain. I love nothing on earth more than my family. However, after spending an entire week in a hotel room with an eight-month-old (rookie mistake), I made a vow that I would never do that again! Of course however, I have since broken that vow, and in hindsight, would do it again a hundred times over. But I must tell you, I was being quite serious in the moment.

When I'm preparing to preach I like to pull away by myself and seek God concerning what He would have me share . . . without any interruptions. With a baby in the mix, that is impossible! Every time I would open my Bible, Judah would come crawling toward me, demanding my full attention. The first couple of times this happened I thought it was cute. However, when he continued crawling back and forth between my wife and I, I knew my level of productivity was going to plummet. Don't write me off. As much as l love my boy, he threw a wrench in my system, and I was getting bothered. I hate to say it but when the week was finished, as wonderful as it was, I was ready to get back to my office—alone!

Then an interesting thing happened. When I was back at the church working in my office, something didn't feel right. I was getting my work done but I was missing something. I was missing the interruptions. I was missing that which just a few days ago felt like an inconvenience. I even missed getting slobbered on. As crazy as it sounds, I sat at my desk with a little smirk, slightly choked up, and thought to myself, "I sure wish Judah was here to bother me right now."

DISTURB US LORD

I have heard my pastor, Keith Nix, share this quote attributed to Sir Francis Drake countless times. It has become one of my favorites. It speaks directly to the heart of what I'm sharing:

> Disturb us, Lord, when
> We are too well pleased with ourselves,
> When our dreams have come true
> Because we have dreamed too little,
> When we arrived safely
> Because we sailed too close to the shore.
> Disturb us, Lord, when
> With the abundance of things we possess
> We have lost our thirst
> For the waters of life;
> Having fallen in love with life,

> We have ceased to dream of eternity
> And in our efforts to build a new earth,
> We have allowed our vision
> Of the new Heaven to dim.
>
> Disturb us, Lord, to dare more boldly,
> To venture on wider seas
> Where storms will show your mastery;
> Where losing sight of land,
> We shall find the stars.
>
> We ask You to push back
> The horizons of our hopes;
> And to push into the future
> In strength, courage, hope, and love.[1]

Will you invite God to come bother you again? Do you dare to pray, "Disturb us, Lord"? Heaven has released a clarion call. Will you join me on this journey? There are giants before us that must fall. But they will not fall by our strength or by our power. They will not fall before men and women who are building their own kingdom. They will only fall before those who have died to self.

There is a reason we have been summoned to be crucified with Christ. We are mere steps away from the apex of history. God has a strategic plan at work, leading us to the very moment where Heaven and earth will yet again intersect. Will you be a part of those who have died to self so that you may be used by God? Turn the page and join me as we journey through the life of a dead man.

CHAPTER 2
THAT'S NOT MY NAME

It doesn't take a prophet to look around and realize that America is in trouble. Whenever a society openly and blatantly celebrates immorality, the desperate need for awakening could not be more clear. This nation has never seen days like this before. While this dark hour may be uncharted territory for the Church it is not uncharted territory for the Lord. He has seen the end from the beginning, and He has a plan.

If you are anything like me, you have had moments where you've looked at the moral bankruptcy that is on full display in our country and in response said to God, "When are You going to do something about this?" I experienced a life defining moment one day when I asked God that very question. He gave me a rather unexpected response. In my spirit I heard the Lord say, "No son, when are *you* going to do something about this?"

Immediately, I wanted to start making excuses. However, the more I meditated on God's response the more I realized one great truth . . . God is not looking for our strength—He is looking for our surrender. That's it. Full surrender to His plan. The classic book, *The Cost of Discipleship* by German theologian Deitrich Bonhoeffer puts it best saying, "When Christ calls a man, He bids him come and die."[1] Dead men have always been God's way of countering darkness in the world. Friend, you and I are God's plan for defeating the deep depravity our generation is facing. I understand that such a bold statement might sound arrogant to some. However, I'm sure you're a lot like me—this reality makes my knees knock. I am well aware that I, alone, am not qualified for this job. Have you ever felt that way? Despite our inadequacies, God has chosen us for this moment in history.

> GOD IS NOT LOOKING FOR OUR STRENGTH. HE IS LOOKING FOR OUR SURRENDER.

HE IS DOING IT AGAIN

Whenever a culture veers off the highway of moral integrity and purposefully plunges into sin, God always counters it with an obscure remnant that cuts against the grain. These messengers do not create comfort, they create conflict. They stand as an undeniable force of opposition to their cultural climate. This is why we are being summoned. God is raising up His remnant as an unstoppable force to withstand the tide of evil crashing down upon our nation.

God has a track record of doing things this way. Before the first coming of Christ, God raised up such a force in a man by the name of John. At the closing of the book bearing his name, the prophet Malachi declared, *"Behold, I will send you Elijah the prophet before the coming of the great and dreadful day of the Lord."* Now fast forward to Matthew 11:14, Jesus said about John the Baptist, *"he is Elijah who is to come."* In God's mercy He raised up this eccentric man, who came in the spirit and power of Elijah, as a forerunner to the Messiah's coming. John was raised as a voice crying in the wilderness, preparing the way of the Lord—calling the world to repentance. I believe that God is doing it again. He is raising up forerunners to prepare the way for His return. He is raising up those who will call the world around them to repentance. But this time He's not just using an individual, He's using all who will say "yes" to His plan. He is using all who will say as John did, *"He must increase but I must decrease."* In other words, He is calling dead men.

THE BIRTH OF A DEAD MAN

John's inception is rather interesting and even parallels with the conflict many of those called to this Kingdom operation are facing today. In Luke 1 we meet John's parents, Zacharias and Elizabeth, who had sought God for a child for many long years. Nevertheless, by the time we are acquainted with them in the first chapter of Luke's gospel, they are well advanced in age and Elizabeth has remained barren throughout that time. One day as Zacharias was serving in the temple, the miraculous happened. An angel appeared to him and said,

> *"Do not be afraid, Zacharias, for your prayer is heard; and your wife Elizabeth will bear you a son, and you shall call his name John." (Luke 1:13)*

Sure enough, that which they had so desperately longed for finally happened. Elizabeth conceived and gave birth to a baby boy. Shortly after his arrival it came time for the baby to be circumcised and named. Following tradition, everyone wanted to name him after his father, Zacharias. Yet, Elizabeth wasn't budging. No doubt she remembered the instruction from Heaven, that they were to name this child John. Despite the pressure of her peers, Elizabeth stuck to her bearings.

Appalled that Elizabeth wanted to name this child John, they turned to Zacharias hoping for a different response. Yet, staying true to the instruction from Heaven, Zacharias too, let them know this child was to be named John. They were shocked!

What a picture this paints. Do you see it? Everyone who is called to prepare the way for the Lord's coming knows what it is like to not fit the mold. The crowd wanted to call John what they thought was best. Yet, God had already spoken something different. The world wanted to identify him one way, while Heaven had already determined to identify him another way.

THAT'S NOT MY NAME

Back when I was in middle school, I was a little bit of a punk. To put things in perspective, over the years as I've bumped into former teachers, they all seem to nearly faint when they hear that I am now a minister of the gospel. If God can redeem me, He can redeem anyone!

I'll never forget one dear teacher, whose buttons I became quite an expert at pushing. Ms. Smith's tolerance level for my shenanigans, on a scale from one to ten, had to be around negative fifteen. At that time in my life it seemed as though the lower the tolerance level of the teacher, the more tempting the situation became. Every day I would come in with a new plan to ruffle her feathers.

For example, one day when she slipped out of the classroom for just a few moments, I ran to her computer and unplugged her mouse. She got so flustered that she assumed it was broken and ended up calling the Tech for technical support! Another time, she had told us that we were going to be watching a video the following day, so I showed up to class early that next morning. While she was out of the room, I turned the volume on the television all the way up, then turned the TV off. When she quieted the class and flipped on the TV, you would have thought she was a professional basketball player. The volume level startled her so badly she jumped nearly three feet in the air!

I feel like I need to repent all over again as I recall these stories. If you ever read this, Ms. Smith, I am sorry! Let me end by sharing the story that takes the cake. I could tell during class one afternoon that Ms. Smith was in a particularly irritable mood for some reason. Needless to say, I was ready to take full advantage of the situation. While she was teaching at the whiteboard, I wrote a note and passed it around to my friends. The note told them that on my cue we would begin softly humming one consistent high pitch note until she turned around, then we would stop. Once she turned back to the whiteboard, we would start again. The plan was genius!

After a couple minutes Ms. Smith was done. She'd had enough! Knowing I was the ringleader she marched over to my desk to render punishment; that's when something rather bizarre took place. As she approached my desk she shouted, "Joe, get in the hall." I thought to myself, "Wait, did she just call me Joe?" So being the punk preteen that I was, I completely ignored her. The closer she came, the louder she shouted, "Joe, I said get in the hall, now!" Again, I didn't know what in the world was up with her calling me Joe, so I just sat there as if she were talking to someone else. Finally, she grabbed me by the arm and drug me to the principal's office.

When we got there and sat down, the principal asked why I persisted in ignoring Ms. Smith. My response, though a lie, even gained a chuckle from the principal. I said, "I didn't know who she was talking to. She kept calling me Joe." To this day I have no idea why she kept calling me Joe! I guess I had just finally pushed her over the edge, and she needed a factory reset! When all was said and done however, I learned my lesson. A few days spent in detention and a whoopin' at home did the trick.

I never tried that stunt again.

THE FIGHT FOR YOUR DESTINY

While I was completely wrong to treat my teacher the way I did, there was a lesson to be learned. I think you and I would be much better off if we would adopt a similar response and refuse to answer to any voice that would call us by any name other than that which our Father has named us. I believe right now there is a war waging for the destiny of those who have been summoned, like John, to be a voice calling our society to repentance. The voice of culture will tell you to blend into your surroundings, to buy into the American dream, to pursue nothing more than a normal life. Then there is the Voice that is roaring from Heaven. It is the voice that is telling you that you were not made for normal, that you will never be satisfied with merely kicking back and ignoring the sin you see in the world around you. Today, you must decide which voice you are going to ignore and which voice you are going to respond to.

Are you going to cower back and follow the culture's lead as they call you something your Father never called you? Or will you refuse to give ear to any voice that is declaring an inferior identity over you? The gospel doesn't call you to the American dream, it calls you to Heaven's dream. You will either respond to Heaven's call and ignore any voice calling you by another name, or you will settle for a false identity and forfeit your Heavenly authority. Choose the name Heaven has declared over you!

If you look at the life of John as he entered into ministry, you will quickly realize he had only one goal—to get his audience to look past him and to see Jesus. God is looking for those who will die to the call of this culture and live for the call of our King. Heaven is bidding us to die so that we may truly live.

CHAPTER 3
RAISING WOLVES

The trumpets of awakening have been silent for too long. It's time to sound the alarm! Where are those who will raise their voice? The message that God has destined to be carried by a generation of firebrands has been hindered. It has been held back due to the compromise-stricken lives of the messengers. Those who are called to be a voice crying in the wilderness have become drunk on a message of lawlessness that has disguised itself as grace. The catastrophic results of God's messengers drinking from the intoxicating well of lawlessness are far more damning than we may realize. Because we have tolerated sin in the Church, we now have a generation that is celebrating sin in the world. We thought we could play it cool and pretend there was a line drawn between the sacred and the sinful that we would never dare negotiate. Yet the world has called our bluff. Our silence towards sin and immorality is deafening. They have watched as we've stood passively on the sidelines while they have continued growing increasingly more progressive in their agenda. They have noticed our hypocrisy, pretending to live one way on Sunday, yet much differently when we think our Christian comrades aren't watching.

How did we veer so far from truth? Where is the influence we once had? Why have the messengers seemingly lost their voice? The answer is simple. Sin became a trivial matter in our hearts and minds.

If you didn't put the book down after reading that last line, you can help turn the ship. You can change the world. You can be a messenger who releases true transformation in the culture around you. Sadly however, most who are called to this strategic assignment check out the moment sin is addressed. In the lives of twenty-first century Christians, anything relating to a holy standard is most often dismissed as legalism, when in fact it is the righteousness of God beckoning us to come up higher in our faith. Too many minds immediately go to a dress code and a list of rules. They dwell on everything they will have to give up, all the while oblivious to the fact that they have walked right into the devil's trap.

You see, the devil knew we could not walk in power without walking in purity. He knew that our strength to speak into the world would never be greater than our separation from the world. He knew that without holiness, we would never accomplish the assignment before us.

> YOU CANNOT WALK IN POWER IF YOU DO NOT WALK IN PURITY.

So he led us to believe that holiness is the enemy, that having any kind of standard means you are legalistic and lack an understanding of God's grace. What he didn't tell you is that revival only travels on the highway of holiness. The only path into the plan of God is one of true surrender. Jesus was very clear. He gave us a roadmap that would get us from where we are, to where He is calling us. He said, *"If anyone desires to come after Me, let him deny himself, and take up his cross daily, and follow Me."* (Luke 9:23)

Holiness always has been and always will be the way of the Kingdom. When we neglect this reality, we negate the power of God in our lives.

There is no doubt in my mind that we are the generation called to right this ship. God is summoning us as a voice that will cry in the wilderness. The spirit of Elijah is being poured out on a people who appear to be the most unlikely of candidates. We are a part of a rather unorthodox crew who will not take the stage to comfort those in complacency. God is putting a voice in us that this generation cannot ignore. Our words will cut to the heart of those who have tethered themselves to a life of compromise.

How then are we to respond to the summoning? Like John the Baptist, we must be a voice that calls the lost to repentance. We must be a people who point the attention away from us and onto Jesus. We must decrease and Christ must increase. You and I must become dead men. Just as John went forth in the spirit and power of Elijah to prepare the way for Jesus, so you and I are coming under the spirit of Elijah to prepare the way for the Lord's return.

THE NEMESIS

As we explore the parallels between Elijah's time and our time, you might be quite stunned. Solomon was exactly right when he wrote that there is nothing new under the sun. Elijah's entrance into scripture is a bit abrupt. He seemingly pops up out of nowhere. In 1 Kings 16 we meet the new ruler of Israel, King Ahab, who had just begun his reign at the time that we are introduced to Elijah. As you read through the storyline, you discover God instated the ministry of Elijah at this particular time in history to combat the wickedness at work through king Ahab and his wife Jezebel, and to address the compromise Israel had become so immersed in. Here's what Elijah was up against:

> *"In the thirty-eighth year of Asa king of Judah, Ahab the son of Omri became king over Israel; and Ahab the son of Omri reigned over Israel in Samaria twenty-two years. Now Ahab the son of Omri did evil in the sight of the LORD, more than all who were before him. And it came to pass, as though it had been a trivial thing for him to walk in the sins of Jeroboam the son of Nebat, that he took as wife Jezebel the daughter of Ethbaal, king of the Sidonians; and he went and served Baal and worshiped him." (1 Kings 16:29-31)*

What depth of evil does someone have to participate in for scripture to record that they were more corrupt than all who had lived before them? Ahab's transgressions before the Lord were no joke. Marrying Jezebel was bad. Worshiping Baal was bad. Yet, these issues are merely symptoms of a far worse disease at work beneath the surface. The most telling thing about Ahab in the verses we just looked at is that he considered sin to be a "trivial" matter.

That sounds a lot like the world we find ourselves in today. What does it matter if the lives we live offend the heart of God? It's no big deal, right? We can always repent later, can't we? Whenever a culture begins to regard sin as a trivial matter, they are headed for destruction.

RAISING THE WRONG PETS

There is a story I once heard about a lady who had a bizarre infatuation with wolves. From the time she was a teenager she simply became fascinated with them. After going through school and graduating college she was finally at a point in life where she could make her long-time dream come true of getting her own house and furthermore—getting pet wolves. Yes, you read that correctly . . . pet wolves.

She ended up with a small litter of baby wolves, which made her wildest dreams a reality. She did all she knew to do to train and domesticate them. Yet, these animals which once appeared to be nothing more than cute pups, grew up. They became strong and powerful. Though she had done all the training and was convinced she had the situation under control, she was sadly mistaken. One day, when she arrived home and went to feed them as she had always done, these seemingly sweet *pet* wolves, who she raised under her care, suddenly snapped as she was going through her normal routine and mauled her to death.

I don't mean to make light of this lady's tragic death. Yet, I think far too many of us have something gravely in common with her. We too are convinced we have the sin epidemic under control. We've tried to domesticate something whose intent is to kill us. Just because we have come to the repulsive position of seeing sin as a trivial matter, doesn't mean that Heaven has. No way. Sin cost Jesus His very blood.

WE CAN'T STAY QUIET

I know it's not popular anymore and we label anyone who dares to speak to this issue as a Pharisee, but dead men can't stay quiet any longer. We have a generation that is celebrating their journey to hell. Because we don't want to offend anyone, we have remained silent on the sidelines and stayed out of the fight. Our society has been convinced they have it under control, but I'm telling you, just like those pet wolves, sin will always turn on you.

If we don't raise our voice, who will? If the remnant does not seek to rescue our world from eternal damnation, will anyone? Genesis 4:7 says, *"Sin is crouching at the door, eager to control you. But you must subdue it and be its master."* (NLT) God is calling for the forerunners. The alarm is sounding. We must raise our voice, make the path straight, and get our generation ready for the return of Christ. How long will you remain silent? You have been chosen as a voice.

CHAPTER 4
CONNECTION CONUNDRUMS

In the last chapter, we began exploring the unbelievable level of corruption taking place in Israel at the time that Elijah came forth as a voice of reckoning. Within a mere handful of verses the wickedness of king Ahab is acknowledged not just once, but twice. To reiterate what we are talking about here, remember that 1 Kings 16:30 says, *"Ahab the son of Omri did evil in the sight of the Lord, more than all who were before him."* and that he, *"did more to provoke the Lord God of Israel to anger than all the kings of Israel who were before him."*

This must have been one messed up brother! He did more to anger the Lord than all the kings who were before him. Think about that statement. That is no small accusation. How does one dive that deeply into corruption? What did Ahab do to become known as Israel's most corrupt king? How did he get so far off track? You could sum it all up with one word: Jezebel.

THE EVOLUTION OF ILLUSTRATIONS

Over the years, my sermon illustrations have evolved depending on what stage of life I'm in. Prior to being married, nearly every story I told to help relate a Kingdom principle revolved around life with family and friends. After getting married, my illustrations shifted to talking about life with my precious wife. Then we got cats and I went an entirely different, rather strange, route. Thank God, He delivered me from that season! And now, since November 13, 2019, I am talking a lot about life as a dad to illustrate my points. I swore I would never be that preacher, but here we are, and I'm past the point of no return!

A few weeks after Judah was born, my wife Ali saw a hilarious meme that said something along these lines, "I carried you for nine long months just for you to come out looking like your dad?!" Hilarious! While I must admit, as time goes on, Judah is increasingly carrying more of his momma's beautiful traits, there is still no denying he is my son.

Anyone who knows my wife knows that you almost have a better chance of getting struck by lightning than you do of catching her without a smile. She is an angel! I have literally caught her smiling in her sleep many times. I, on the other hand, have been told on more than a few occasions that I apparently have what many refer to as resting jerk face—not the most flattering compliment I've ever received. While most of the time I am genuinely beaming on the inside, pictures have proven time and time again that unless I remind myself to smile, I look as though I am mad at the world. Without realizing it, I tend to squint my eyes and furrow my brows when I'm not intentionally making myself smile, and especially when I'm in deep thought. Ali and I even have a long-standing joke where she'll reach over and rub my forehead saying, "Loosen up and look happy."

Well, it was all fun and games until Judah came along, squinting his eyes and furrowing his brows! After nine months of being carried in his momma's womb he still came out bearing a few of my signature mannerisms. I didn't have to teach them to him. Nor was he trained to look like me. Nevertheless, my precious, handsome boy entered the world with—well, in the words of what others have said to me . . . resting jerk face.

Judah may have come from the queen of smiles, but there is no denying that he caught a few things from his Pop. What's the point? What you give birth to reveals what you have been intimate with.

WHAT YOU GIVE BIRTH TO REVEALS WHAT YOU HAVE BEEN INTIMATE WITH.

CONNECTIONS DETERMINE DIRECTION

All the corruption that was birthed in Israel during the reign of King Ahab comes down to the fact that he was intimate with Jezebel. Whether it be for good or for evil, such as it was for Ahab, your connections are determining the direction of your life. Those who you allow to take a seat at the table of your heart will either ensnare you or empower you. There is no middle ground.

In Luke's recording of the gospel, we get an interesting look at the way Jesus went about appointing the twelve apostles. It was no frivolous matter, but rather quite the opposite,

> *"Now it came to pass in those days that He went out to the mountain to pray and continued all night in prayer to God. And when it was day, He called His disciples to Himself; and from them He chose twelve whom He also named apostles."* (Luke 6:12-13)

Wait a minute. Why did Jesus, the Son of God, spend an entire night praying before appointing the twelve men with whom He would spend most of His time? I can assure you that it was not because He did not know how to select the right inner circle. Could it be perhaps that He knew we would not know how to select the right inner circle? Maybe His process was revealed to set a pattern we could follow.

How much different would our lives look if we spent the night in prayer seeking God's heart on whom we allow to live within close proximity to us? Please don't misunderstand what I am trying to communicate. I am not advocating that we, as disciples of Christ, live in a little bubble and only allow a select few "super-Christians" to have a place in our lives. No way! We could never prepare the way for Christ's coming with that mentality. What I am saying is that if Jesus was that intentional about those He placed closest to Him, shouldn't we be also?

If we were more intentional about seeking God's will concerning how far we allow certain relationships to progress, we would have far fewer preachers caught up in affairs. If we chose the Jesus model, our reputation would cease to be one of hypocrisy and would rather become one of integrity. If we would seek God in prayer before building binding connections, we would have less Christians living double lives. If we stopped carelessly joining our lives to those who are running in the opposite direction, we could get back to influencing the culture that has sadly been influencing us.

It's time that we get smart about who we are partnering with. After all, what fellowship does light have with darkness? One faulty connection resulted in Ahab being labeled as the most corrupt King Israel had ever known. Why did Jesus give us such an extreme model to follow for our most tight-knit relationships? Because you will always become like those you are closest to.

THE COST OF CONNECTIONS

One of the best experiences Ali and I have had thus far in life has been watching our parents become grandparents. They have been absolutely amazing to us and our little guy. Thankfully, we all live fairly close to one another, so they are all a major part of Judah's life—and hey, what new parent doesn't love free babysitting?

Because of my parent's schedule, Judah gets to spend a lot of time with them during the day. It has been such a joy watching him develop a special bond with my mom and dad. This journey has already created unforgettable memories and stories we will tell for a lifetime. Let me give you one humorous example that we often chuckle over now, though at first it had me a bit concerned. One evening while Ali, Judah, and I were all home relaxing I noticed that anytime Judah would stand up from a sitting position on the floor he would let out a little groan like he was in pain. The first time he did it I didn't think much of it, but as it continued throughout the night, I started to get a little worried.

A few days passed, and one evening I went to pick Judah up from my parent's house. He and my dad were sitting on the floor playing, and as soon as I walked through the door Judah stood up, did the concerning groan he had been doing, and came running over to me. Just as I reached down to pick him up, I noticed out of the corner of my eye that my dad was climbing up off the floor. Suddenly, I heard that same familiar groan coming out of his mouth that I had been hearing for days back home. Judah had been copying my dad the entire time! I hope you're catching it. We become like those we are connected to.

WE BECOME LIKE THOSE WE ARE CONNECTED TO.

DEVELOP OR DISMANTLE

As we travel this road together, here is a question we must all be willing to ask—what relationships have I developed that I need to dismantle? I have watched far too many people miss what God longed to do in their lives because they refused to wave goodbye to voices that were steering them in the wrong direction —voices of doubt, compromise, safety, jealousy, you name it. So, I must ask; what influence have you given yourself to that has the potential of holding you back from the destiny God has in store for your life? Living the life of a dead man means that your supreme *yes* to the call of God also means an unwavering *no* to any voice that is at war with Heaven's plan for your life.

CHAPTER 5
WIND & FIRE

Have you ever done something so utterly embarrassing that the only appropriate way to respond was to just hit it head-on and own it? You know what I mean, a blunder so bad that it will forever be etched into the corridors of your mind, with absolutely no hope of ever being erased. If so, you are not alone. There have been too many times that those in my inner circle have had a good laugh at the expense of my bruised ego. Unfortunately for me, I don't have just one or two isolated incidents to reminisce . . . I have a whole list pointing back from life's rear-view mirror.

In January of 2018 I had one such experience that topped the charts. Christmas was over and our families had completely spoiled us. Our home was overflowing with gifts! They went over the top. Once everything was unpacked and put away, we moved all the cardboard boxes into the garage.

After a few weeks went by, having put off taking the boxes to the dump, I finally quit procrastinating and decided to clear them out. As I started to load them into my car, I quickly realized I was going to need a truck for this haul. So I called my dad and asked to borrow his truck. He agreed, but then suggested what sounded like an easier, and much more entertaining option. He suggested that I just burn them in my fire pit. I don't know why I hadn't thought of that! I am a borderline pyromaniac, so I loved the idea of getting to play with fire.

I jumped in, dismantled all the boxes, and got to it. There was a lot more cardboard than I had realized. At one point, when the fire was at its peak, the wind slightly picked up, making me a little nervous. With each gust of wind, pieces of burning cardboard were carried away. I watched as each piece started heading straight for my house and the houses surrounding ours. So I quickly grabbed the water hose and drenched everything in sight just to be on the safe side.

After a thorough soaking there were still a few smoldering embers shining through the ashes. So I asked Ali to keep an eye on what was happening while I hopped in the shower. Only moments had passed when Ali came running into the bathroom yelling, "The fire is blazing outside!"

Thinking she was kidding, I asked, "Are you serious?" She didn't even acknowledge my question. In a panic she yelled, "What should I do?!" Noticing the anxiety in her voice, I knew it was a big deal. I shouted, "Run out there and drench it with the hose!" Off she went, wasting no time. With my heart racing a million beats a minute, I wasn't thinking straight. I knew I needed to scope the severity of the fire and see if it was indeed blazing. Soaking wet, I jumped out of the shower and ran for the window, not even bothering to grab a towel. Our floor was soaked!

Sure enough when I got out of our bathroom and over to our bedroom window to look outside, the fire wasn't just blazing . . . It was raging! While watching the flames leap higher and higher, I looked over and saw Ali just standing there, near the flames, with nothing more than a trickle dripping from the end of the hose. There was apparently a kink somewhere in the line and she was too flustered to figure it out. It was as if she were fighting a forest fire with a water pistol! Beating on the window to get her attention, I started screaming, "Unkink the hose! Unkink the hose! We are about to burn the house down!" She shouted back, "I can't hear you! Help! I'm scared Babe!"

With no time to lose, I sprung into action, and this is where things get embarrassing. Ringing wet, and without a stitch of clothes on, I took off running through our house! By the time I took the turn into the kitchen headed for the backdoor, I slipped and fell. It hurt like the dickens, but I jumped up and kept going. There would be time to lick my wounds later. Running out the backdoor, I ripped the hose out of Ali's hands and shouted, "Help me! Go find the kink!"

What did Ali do in response? As I stood there with a water hose that barely had a trickle coming out of it, next to flames that were leaping six feet high, less than a few steps from our home, Ali stood there with her legs crossed, laughing so hard she was crying! I continued shouting, "Help! Help!" Through tears, Ali said, "Stop! I'm about to pee! Where are your clothes?!"

Oh. My. Gosh.

I went streaking in my backyard . . . unintentionally I must add. Listen, we live in a neighborhood where homes are fairly close together. We have a privacy fence surrounding our property, but the homes behind us are a bit elevated. My neighbors had a crystal-clear view of my backside, and everything that went down that fateful night! They got a front row seat to the entire fiasco — they saw the raging fire, my wife who wasn't any help because she was so tickled by the situation, and me, the soaking wet streaker.

No doubt, this was the blunder of all blunders. I was humiliated when Ali pointed out what I had done. I was so flustered by everything that had happened that I didn't even notice I had not put on any clothes! In sheer embarrassment, I bet I turned a shade of red that was new to mankind that night.

For everyone who may be wondering . . . Yes, Ali was able to find the kink, free the hose, and put out the fire. As for me, I did the walk of shame back into our house. I was so humiliated that I didn't even care if it burned anymore! What a night. Ali took advantage of my misfortune for the rest of the evening. She laughed for hours. Her laughter would temporarily subside, then randomly recur again and again, all through the night. Every moment that she reflected upon the humiliating and unfortunate chain of events that had unfolded, laughter would burst forth all over again—and again, and again, all night long.

SETTING THE STAGE

The last thing we discover before Elijah steps onto the stage in the book of 1 Kings might be one of the most disturbing discoveries of all. The embers of evil that had been smoldering in Israel were fanned into a raging wildfire under the rule of Ahab. When sin is considered nothing more than a trivial issue, the flames of corruption will run rampant.

The final verse of 1 Kings 16 records these words,

> "In his days Hiel of Bethel built Jericho. He laid its foundation with Abiram his firstborn, and with his youngest son Segub he set up its gates, according to the word of the LORD, which He had spoken through Joshua the son of Nun." (1 Kings 16:34)

So here we have a guy from Bethel, which is defined as the house of God, who set himself to rebuild Jericho. I'm sure you remember Jericho's history. It's the place where Israel marched around the city just before God miraculously brought down the walls. With that in mind, think about what Hiel of Bethel actually did. He rebuilt what God destroyed. Unfortunately, I don't think Hiel is the only person from the house of God that has sought to rebuild what God has destroyed.

If there is anything we have hopefully learned over the past few years, it is that God is waging war against every counterfeit kingdom that is posing as His Church.

He is showing His perfect jealousy. He is waging war on celebrity Christianity, even bringing once thriving churches to the point of empty auditoriums. He is waging war on the pseudo glory we've been hosting, by teaching us that neither LED screens, nor smoke and lights, will ever be able to take the place of His presence. He is personally knocking down the walls that have stood so strong and tall in our postmodern version of Christianity, as He reveals His jealous love for His bride.

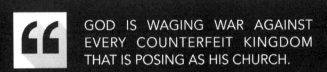

> GOD IS WAGING WAR AGAINST EVERY COUNTERFEIT KINGDOM THAT IS POSING AS HIS CHURCH.

Yet, there remains those like Hiel of Bethel who are desperately trying to rebuild what we have watched God destroy. Sadly, they are not the ones who pay the greatest price for this unthinkable atrocity. Remember, the verse said, *"He laid its foundation with Abiram his firstborn, and with his youngest son Segub he set up its gates."* In other words, rebuilding what God had destroyed cost him the lives of his sons. Don't you see an eerily similar parallel happening in the church that is trying to rebuild what God is waging war on? It is costing us the upcoming generation. If what you are building is costing you what you are called to birth, then you are building the wrong thing.

Why are more and more of those who make up this generation turning away from the Lord? Why are they leaving the Church? Why are the flames of immorality raging at a greater degree now than at any other point in this generation? It is because every emerging generation celebrates what the generation before them tolerates. It's because we have been building the wrong kingdom. We've tried to build something that looks like the world while God is calling us to build something that looks like Heaven on earth. We have not been advancing the plans of God. We've been advancing the plans of man.

THE WIND IS BLOWING

It is time for dead men to take the stage, pointing the world past them and toward Jesus. It is time for the Elijahs to come forth and say enough is enough! If the winds of corruption could fan the flames of immortality happening under Ahab's reign into a wildfire, just think what the winds of revival will do to the embers burning within the hearts of the remnant that is rising. As you look across this nation your soul may be vexed with hopelessness, but I want to encourage you—the wind of the Spirit is blowing, and we are about to see the fires of revival sweep across this land. Heaven has strategically planted firebrands throughout this generation. You and I are a part of them. We may appear to be nothing more than embers in the ashes right now, but if my humiliating situation taught me anything it is that just a little wind can turn a smoldering ember into a raging fire. Dead men are stepping onto the scene and the fires of revival are starting to rage!

CHAPTER 6
DANGERS OF THE DARK

I'm sure you are seeing some undeniable parallels between where we find ourselves as a nation and where Israel was under the rule of Ahab and Jezebel. Just as it was for them, we too are living in a culture that is openly pursing greater depths of corruption than at any other time in our history. It's as though there is an insatiable thirst for anything that might arouse the anger of God. Nevertheless, as I've already said, there is a plan. Darkness always seems to reach new heights right before the light breaks through. When the page turns from 1 Kings 16 over to 1 Kings 17, something dramatic happens. The prophet Elijah is introduced.

Men and women of such resilience are nearly unheard of in our day. Elijah's first words recorded in 1 Kings 17 are, *"As the LORD God of Israel lives, before whom I stand, there shall not be dew nor rain these years, except at my word."* Seemingly out of nowhere this obscure servant of the Lord steps on the scene with the audacity to stand before the wicked king and declare a drought in response to the heinous compromise that had overtaken the land. There is only one way such courage can be obtained. Elijah had nothing to fear because he had nothing to lose. He was living his life as a dead man.

The weight of his unveiling is far more significant than one might initially realize. This man would set a precedent that would stand until the second coming of

Christ. The spirit of Elijah is not about a person, it is about a pattern. Elijah was given as a template. What God did in him, He would later do in John the Baptist as the precursor to Christ's first coming. Now, I believe, God is doing it again in His remnant to prepare the way for Christ's return.

THE PATTERN

In days of great darkness God has a history of raising up voices that come in the spirit of Elijah. They burst onto the scene to right the wrongs of society and straighten the paths that have become crooked. Whenever God wants to prepare a people for His arrival, He summons a remnant that will walk under the conviction of this extraordinary mandate. The life of Elijah lays out a pattern for all who are hungry to see revival in the Church and awakening in the world. Throughout history many have mistakenly made the man their pattern. They've tried to emulate his personality. They've tried to take on his austere demeanor. In doing so they have missed the point. This is not about the man, it's about the mission.

Did you notice that despite his significance, Elijah was not introduced with a lot of fanfare? We don't find him bombarded by an entourage of faithful followers. When we meet him, he isn't passing out business cards or marketing his latest book. He's not jockeying for new followers on social media. He is simply doing what the Lord told him to do. Elijah was not looking to build his kingdom and lead Israel to join themselves to him in great loyalty. Rather, he sounded the alarm and came as a voice from Heaven, seeking to lead Israel to a place of unwavering loyalty to God.

Who will call our crooked society to repentance? Who among us will raise their voice to prepare a people for the Lord's return? Who will stand as a burning lamp in the darkest night of our nation's history? God has given us a pattern that is proven to work.

I believe Elijah's uncanny introduction paints a prophetic picture of what is happening in this very hour. We've watched as darkness has escalated more and more in our society. Our hearts have been cut to the core as our culture celebrates everything from same-sex marriage to the murdering of innocent babies in the womb. The remnant has cried out in despair, "How long will you allow this to persist Lord?" I want to tell you that the day of reckoning has come. Can God trust you to be His hands and feet? Will you allow Him to afflict your soul with an unceasing burden to see this generation turn back to Him? Nothing short of total surrender will work.

John Wesley, the great revivalist, has been credited with saying, "Give me one hundred preachers who fear nothing but sin and desire nothing but God, and I care not whether they be clergymen or laymen, they alone will shake the gates of Hell and set up the kingdom of Heaven upon Earth."[1] If you are wondering what kind of person the eyes of the Lord are searching for right now, John Wesley cut to the chase. To be an Elijah in a world that is spellbound by modern day Ahabs and Jezebels, you can no longer treat fear like a friend, nor sin like a companion. You must die to self.

> WE CAN NO LONGER TREAT FEAR LIKE A FRIEND, NOR SIN LIKE A COMPANION.

BOLDNESS AND BLESSINGS

Before you take another step in this direction we need to talk about the destination of this pathway. I must tell you; this journey is not all glitz and glamour. If you're in it for the wrong reason, you are wasting your time. The faint of heart desiring to take a nice cushy ride to Heaven won't make the cut.

Look at the first few verses of Elijah's life and trade places with him for a moment. How would you expect God to honor your radical boldness as His servant? You would think that Elijah's extreme obedience would immediately lead to extreme blessing. However, after he declared the drought, the word of the Lord came to him saying,

> *"Get away from here and turn eastward, and hide by the Brook Cherith, which flows into the Jordan. And it will be that you shall drink from*

the brook, and I have commanded the ravens to feed you there." (1 Kings 17:3-4)

To be completely honest, this gets me a little bit. I feel kind of bad for Elijah. He just had the courage to put his neck on the line by confronting the king and now this is how he's repaid. He had to run away, drink from the brook Cherith, and eat whatever the ravens brought him. Talk about a blow to moral!

If you just read this instruction on the surface, you might miss some of the rich revelation that is waiting to be uncovered. For example, the brook he was sent to, Cherith, in the original language comes from a word that means cutting.[2] Anyone who has ever said yes to the call of God is familiar with the Holy Spirit drawing them to a similar place. Even those who are courageous enough to stick their finger in the face of a corrupt king must still drink from the brook of cutting and allow God to further chisel them into His image. Your sacrifice will never take the place of your surrender. No matter how you are used by God, He will always love you enough to cut away anything in your life that does not look like Him.

Secondly, and what I really want to draw your attention to as we close this chapter, is that the text tells us God employed ravens to feed Elijah. The prophet of God sure wasn't eating a five-star meal during his stay at the brook Cherith! What's fascinating about this little detail is that if you do any research on the raven species one of the first things you will discover is that these birds are thieves.[3] They'll rob you blind!

Yet, in this story the thief was not going to take from Elijah, Elijah was going to take from the thief. Please don't miss this next point. We too are letting the thief know that he can no longer take anything from us. Furthermore, we are putting him on notice that we are coming to take back everything he has previously stolen. Dead men are raising their voices! We will no longer tolerate the thief plundering our generation. So, the question is, how do we actually make this happen? The first step to stopping the enemy in his tracks begins with how we respond to the darkness.

LIGHT IT UP

Before Ali and I got married, while she was still living with her parents, their house got broken into. It happened one weekend while her mom and dad were away on a camping trip. Ali and a friend were in the home alone and were awakened in the middle of the night by noise coming from the basement. A few moments later they heard someone coming up the stairs, so they ran to hide in the closet.

Thankfully when the burglar heard them running to the closet, he got startled and ran out of the house. Ali's friend called her dad, who happened to be in law enforcement, and he rushed over immediately. When he got there the front door was standing wide open from where the intruder apparently ran out of the house in a hurry. After he cleared the area and the girls came out of hiding, he got every detail they could give on the incident. In the course of the conversation, he made a statement which Ali later told me; one I will never forget. He said the burglar had most likely been studying their home for a while. When he saw that the camper was gone and all the lights were out, he must have assumed he was safe to make a move. The friend's father then said that in the future they should always leave some lights on when they are away because light will usually deter thieves.

I can tell you why the enemy has been so successful in stealing from us all this time. He has studied our lives long and hard. He knows our weak points. He knows our flaws and failures. However, the key to his unfortunate success in robbing from the Church has not been due to his study of our day-to-day journey. It is due, rather, to the reality that our lights have been out. When the Church lives in darkness, the devil wreaks havoc upon the world.

If we don't shine in darkness, the enemy will continue entangling those that see no glimmer of hope among God's people. The emerging generation will further denounce Christianity as they're lured into hell's ploy. We must shake ourselves! We must turn up the light lest we allow the enemy to charge ahead unopposed. God is calling us to shine in the darkest night our nation has ever witnessed. It's now or never!

Our *yes* to Heaven's plan isn't meant to take place just for a moment. It must take place for a lifetime. We can no longer give our adversary room to steal from us. As we choose to give our lives as a living sacrifice to the Lord, you can rest assured He, in return, will keep the fire on the altar so that our lives are always lit. When we burn in darkness, the world will come running to the light.

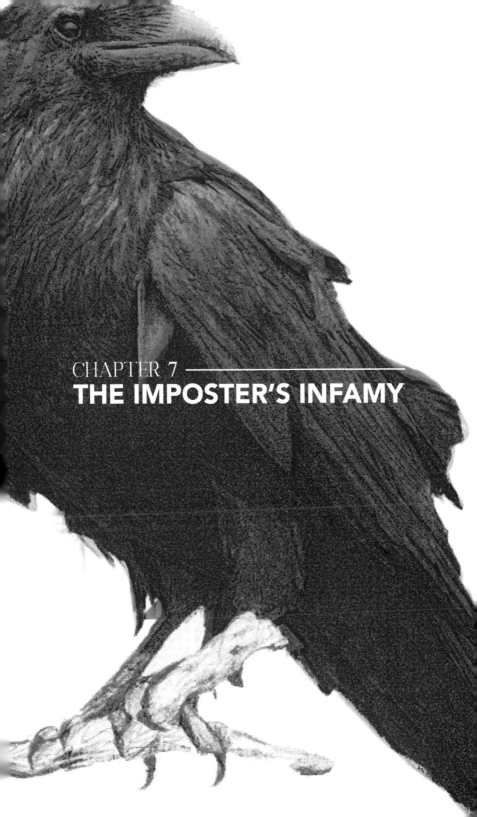

CHAPTER 7
THE IMPOSTER'S INFAMY

In the last chapter we began looking at the obscure, or perhaps I should say, downright strange way God chose to sustain the prophet Elijah during Israel's drought. God didn't exactly roll out the red carpet for him after he spoke as Heaven's mouthpiece against Israel's corrupt culture. Think about this. The God who gave Joseph the prophetic strategy that would sustain Egypt and its neighbors during a seven-year famine; the God who made water gush out of a rock and manna fall from Heaven while Israel wondered through the wilderness; that same God, when it came to Elijah's survival, did not pull any strings nor perform any awe-inspiring stunt for Elijah. He instead called on some filthy ravens to take the man of God breakfast and dinner each day. Really? Ravens? He could have at least sent the food via DoorDash or Grubhub! While I'm writing with a little tongue-in-cheek, I actually do believe God had a specific strategy in feeding Elijah the way that He did.

Ravens are brilliant creatures. As a matter of fact, they are considered one of the most intelligent members among the bird species.[1] They have many fascinating traits such as the uncanny ability to mimic. Whether it be imitating the human language or mimicking a wild animal, ravens are incredible imposters.[2]

If there is anything the modern Church has in common with ravens it is that we too have become experts at imitation. We know how to play the part without ever living the life. The chasm between the lives we are called to live and the way we actually do live, seems to increase day by day. While the American Church continues living under the false pretense of a more socially acceptable gospel, our world is growing increasingly desperate for something real.

THE QUESTION OF THE CURIOUS

Years ago, my pastor encouraged me to listen to a preacher who has since become one of my all-time favorite gospel orators. I'll never forget the very first message I heard from Bishop Kenneth Ulmer. In his sermon he told the story of a little boy who lived in a rundown city just a few blocks from a neighborhood church. Though he lived just blocks away, this young man had never been to church before in his life. He had an insatiable curiosity, constantly pondering what might be happening beneath that old wooden steeple.

One day as he was riding his bicycle, he came near the old neighborhood church and saw the pastor outside doing some landscaping. Still a good distance off, the curious little boy began to shout, "Mister! Mister! Wait a minute!" He continued shouting while pedaling with all of his might towards the church. The pastor, who had worked a long, hard day, turned toward the child and gave him a nod, acknowledging that he would wait for him. The pastor stood patiently waiting until the young boy finally pulled onto the front lawn. Immediately the child picked back up on the conversation. Panting for breath the boy continued, "Mister, mister, can I ask you a question?"

As the minister opened his mouth to respond, the little boy said, "Please! Please! Please! I promise it won't take long. Just one question!" Now chuckling, the pastor motioned for the boy to quiet down, and said to him, "Why sure son. What's your question?" After a long pause, with a sheepish look on his face and eyes wide open, the little boy looked toward the church, "Mister . . . does God live in there?"

The seasoned man of God, now old and gray, having served the Lord as the pastor of this local assembly for many decades, dropped his head. He took a deep breath, then let out a big sigh. Still having yet to respond, he looked up and locked eyes with the young boy. Now staring intently into the big brown eyes of the child, the pastor let out another sigh, shook his head and replied, "You know son, sometimes I wonder."

Unfortunately, I know exactly why the pastor in this story responded the way he did. Too often, those who claim the name of Christ do not practice what they preach. The lives they live betray the words they speak. They have become prolific at talking the talk while never actually walking the walk. Today many Christians want to walk in God's blessing without obeying God's voice. Sadly, the person you see for an hour on Sunday may not be the person you encounter at any other point throughout the week. Their life is just as broken and messed up after they "got saved" as it was before they "got saved".

What grieves the heart of God no longer grieves the heart of His Church. It seems we've replaced holiness with hypocrisy. We have settled for a life of imitation when the true gospel leads us to a life of transformation. This should not be! Since we have settled for a half-hearted gospel, the Church is now producing nothing more than halfhearted Christians. We keep inviting people to pray a prayer while conveniently forgetting to mention that Jesus invites us to come and die. Anything less than joining Christ at the cross will result in living as an imposter.

ANYTHING LESS THAN JOINING CHRIST AT THE CROSS WILL RESULT IN LIVING AS AN IMPOSTER.

CLAIM VS CONDUCT

It has been recorded that before rising to power, Adolf Hitler said in a campaign speech, "We want to fill our culture again with the Christian Spirit."[3] Of course, as we look back over history, the Holocaust proves that this demonized tyrant's claim was at odds with his conduct. The subtle whisper of hypocrisy is one of the greatest enemies of the soul. It spares no one in its pursuit of destruction. When we settle for anything less than true transformation, we will live subject to the tyrannical rule of pretension. Our enemy longs for nothing more than for the Church to claim one thing and live another. Why? In the Kingdom of God, imposters make no lasting impact. We cannot bring change to the world around us, if the world around us sees no change within us.

I am not mad at those who have fallen prey to the trap of living as an imposter. I am not mad at those who have settled for a counterfeit faith. I am grieved for them. I am grieved for the lives they could be reaching. Knowing firsthand what it is like to live as a slave to compromise and sin, I can tell you that putting on a show will never bring relief. Living life on the never-ending treadmill of performance will only leave you empty and defeated. My heart breaks for those caught in this trap, not just because I have been in their shoes, but more importantly, my heart breaks for them because I know what they are missing. I know what it is like to be transformed by the gospel. Jesus was not lying when He said, *"If the Son makes you free, you shall be free indeed."* *(John 8:36)* The true gospel brings true change. You don't have to live feverishly *trying* to be a Christian. No, the gospel doesn't invite you to try harder. It invites you to die. Colossians 2:20 says, *"You have died with Christ, and He has set you free from the spiritual powers of this world." (NLT)* This is the kind of Church our culture so desperately needs to see — a people who no longer live for themselves, but a people who have died with Christ.

HAS IT WORKED FOR YOU?

Let me tell you about a horrific experience my friends had. After many years of being happily married, they found themselves facing an extremely difficult season. Life had just knocked the wind out of their sail, and they were struggling to keep their relationship alive. Marital bliss had come to a screeching halt. So, they decided it was time to take the fight for their love to the next level. They sought out professional help by enrolling in marriage counseling. I believe this is a noble and commendable move for any marriage facing hardships. There was however one problem—they hired the wrong marriage counselor.

After a few weeks, my friends noticed that they were leaving each session in worse shape than when they arrived. The counselor was well aware of their lack of progress and decided to "change up" his strategy. He requested to meet with them individually before all coming together again. Revering him as the professional, they agreed to go along with his plan.

The husband was up first. Now, understand, he was serious about fighting for his marriage, but he had not been impressed with this particular counselor from day one. Nevertheless, he went for his individual appointment. That meeting turned out to be the straw that broke the camel's back.

As the session began, they dove into the conflict from the husband's perspective, and then, the counselor gave him some advice that just pushed him over the edge. After listening to my friend share from a place of utter desperation, the counselor responded, "I think it's time you just put your foot down and tell your wife like it is."

Baffled by the counselor's statement, my friend responded almost involuntarily, "Are you crazy?! I'm trying to save my marriage, not destroy it!" Still in shock from what he had just heard he continued, "Man, this all sounds like a bunch of bull—does your wife actually take this garbage?" The counselor, taken back a bit, began fumbling for words. Finally, pointing to himself he responded, "Oh me? No, uh I'm not married."

As if the situation couldn't get any worse, the counselor continued by saying, "My wife left me a few years ago." That was it. My friend had heard enough! He got up and walked out!

THE END OF PRETENDING

I guess by now you have probably figured out the story you just read is complete fiction. It never happened. By the time you read those last few lines I'm sure you knew it wasn't true. Who in their right mind would follow someone with that kind of pedigree? Yet, I'm afraid the American church too often looks like a marriage counselor who is reeling from a fifth failed marriage, or a financial coach filing for bankruptcy. Our society does not care if we can fill auditoriums if they see no changed lives. Shallow Christians have played the role of an imposter for far too long. We cannot try to *pretend* our way out of the problem. Until the world sees that the gospel has changed us, why would they ever want to see if it can change them?

> UNTIL THE WORLD SEES THAT THE GOSPEL HAS CHANGED US, WHY WOULD THEY EVER WANT TO SEE IF IT CAN CHANGE THEM?

How do we close the chasm between our claim and our conduct? How do we rid the Church of the imposter mentality that's held us in a death grip for so long? We must be crucified with Christ. Our sphere of influence needs more than imitation. They need to see transformation. As long as there is a gap between what we preach and what we practice, we forfeit our authority to release cultural change. This isn't about what we bring to the table. It's about what we nail to the cross. It's time to put the mask away and let grace work in our lives.

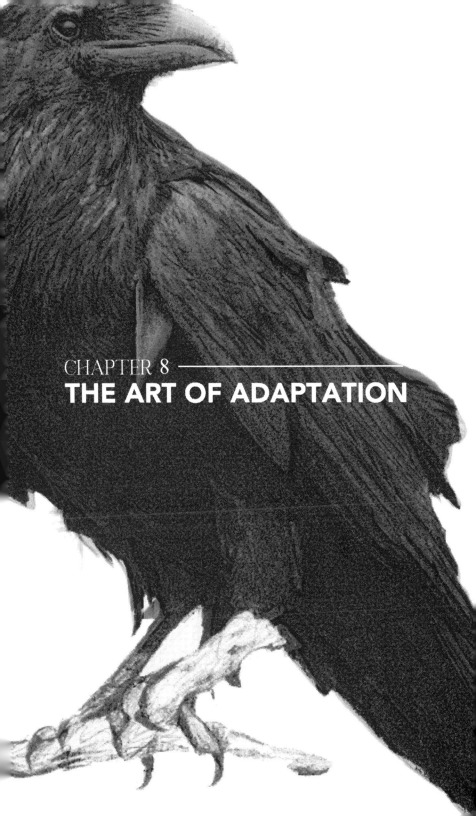

CHAPTER 8
THE ART OF ADAPTATION

During my teen years I fell in love with the Bible. You have no idea how out of character that was for me! Growing up I was never much of a reader. In all honesty, I hated reading. When I was in middle school, we were required to read a minimum of one book every six weeks and then visit the library to take a quiz on the book we had chosen. We could take the quiz whenever we wanted on our own time. We just had to go to the library, enter our student I.D. into the computer and complete the quiz. Upon passing, our quota was met for that six weeks. If we did not pass, we had to read another book and try again. Just so you understand how badly I hated reading—the only way I was able to meet those requirements was by bribing my friends to go to the library, enter my student I.D. and do the quiz for me. I was quite the chump!

Something changed when I started really digging into the gospels. The Word began to come alive, and I couldn't put it down. During that first year I believe I ended up reading both testaments, old and new, cover to cover, for the first time in my life and I have been hooked ever since. In doing this, I discovered something... the Bible has some strange things in it.

How about that awkward moment when Balaam started beating his donkey? As if that isn't odd enough, the donkey responded verbally... with words... to Balaam's outburst of rage by saying, *"What have I done to you that deserves your beating me three times?"*

Then Balaam proceeded to argue with his donkey as if there was nothing abnormal about the two of them bickering back and forth. (Numbers 22:21-31 NLT)

Or what about the time that Elijah's protégé, Elisha, got so bent out of shape over some kids yelling, *"Go away, Baldy"* that he cursed them, and two bears came from the woods and mauled the children to death? I guess he showed them! (2 Kings 2:23-24 NLT)

And how about the prophetic instruction God gave to Isaiah to go around naked for three years as a symbol of the terrible troubles to come? (See Isaiah 20:3)

Just to name a few . . .

The Bible is full of these little oddities. That is probably one of the reasons I love it so much. The deeper you dig, the more interesting things become. While God feeding Elijah via the ravens certainly makes the list of such strange occurrences you find in scripture, I'm really not all that shocked by this choice. Think about it. God did not have to do too much tweaking in their little heads to cause the ravens to spot this prophet. What we see with Elijah is the prototype of a dead man. Why should we be surprised that ravens were able to find him? Isn't their species drawn to dead things anyway?

THE CULTURE OF CONFORMITY

I want to look at one last interesting trait you will discover about ravens as you research their unique attributes. These birds can live in nearly any climate. They have mastered the art or adaptation. With that in mind, let me ask you a question. Thus far in the story who do you think the American Church more accurately identifies with — Elijah the prophet, who stood out amongst corrupt Israel as a light in darkness, or the ravens, who are masters at adapting to their environment?

For far too long, I believe we have identified more with the nature of the raven than we have the nature of Elijah. It seems we merely conform to whatever we are surrounded by. The sad reality is that many Christians have also mastered the art of adaptation. We've come to a place where the churches we consider most cutting edge are not the ones who stand out but rather blend in with culture.

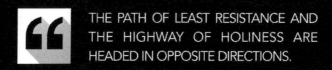

THE PATH OF LEAST RESISTANCE AND THE HIGHWAY OF HOLINESS ARE HEADED IN OPPOSITE DIRECTIONS.

Why have we settled for a lack of influence? We have forfeited our Kingdom mandate to shape culture and bring Heaven to earth. Too many who are called to be the voice of one crying in the wilderness have instead embraced the nature of the raven. We have chosen that which is easy over that which is right. The path of least resistance and the highway of holiness are headed in opposite directions. God is beckoning His people to choose the right path!

There is a price to be paid for all who refuse to conform to the environment around them. We live in a "cancel culture" world. Let me warn anyone who may think that the path ahead for those who oppose darkness will be easy—it won't. Make no mistake; you will be ridiculed and mocked. You will be labeled as intolerant and deemed as a bigot for refusing to buy into their redefining of love and tolerance. But if you are going to be a part of the company that is preparing the way for the return of the Lord, you must brace yourself. It will not make life easy, but it is the only thing really worth living for. The alternative is to simply accept their initiative and go with the flow.

If you are ok with living under the nature of the raven then you should have no problem with the death culture that is being presented to us in this hour. You should have no problem with the fact that we live in a nation that celebrates "our legal right" to slaughter the unborn. You should have no problem with the reality that children are being brainwashed into believing that their gender identity is fluid and they may change it at the drop of a hat. You should have no problem with the fact that they want sex outside of marriage to be the accepted and celebrated social norm. Furthermore, you should have no problem with their idea that all sexual restrictions should be removed. In their mind love is love and it doesn't matter if that means it is between two men, or a man and a child, or any other abominable, unimaginable combination.

If you are ok living with the same nature that ravens have, you will have no problem adapting with these issues. However, if you are going to live with the nature of Elijah, these issues pose a serious problem that must be addressed. What we are rapidly discovering is that our morally deprived culture is demanding that everyone choose a side. But they are not the only ones issuing a demand. Heaven is calling us to attention. God is looking for His chosen ones who will stand like Elijah, stick their finger in the face of corruption, and say enough is enough.

Which nature will you choose? Will you stand as an Elijah, or will you blend in as a raven?

STAY IN THE LIGHT

Let me tell you about one of the most disappointing moments I experienced as a child. I had saved my allowance for over three weeks in anticipation of going to the store with my mom and dad. You see, during that time, everyone was coming to school with really cool glow-in-the-dark necklaces. It had become the new fad and I had to be a part of it. After saving and saving, one Friday afternoon payday finally rolled around, and I had enough to buy the necklace I had so badly wanted. That evening we took a trip to the store, and I spent my hard-earned money so that I could join the fad. I was so excited!

As soon as we got in the car, I ripped that package open and snapped the necklace around my neck. In my mind, I had now arrived. My life on cloud nine, however, was short-lived. After only a few short hours, my necklace was already starting to dim. I was furious! It had only been a few hours—and it was just Friday. There was no way it would last until Monday so that I could wear it to school. I felt gypped!

When I complained about it to my parents, my dad told me that if I would set it under my lamp for a few hours it would get its glow back. Though I must admit that I didn't believe him, he made a believer out of me. I did just as he said and sure enough after a few hours of sitting under my lamp, that necklace was glowing again.

I believe I know why so many in the Church today identify more with the raven than they do with Elijah. We no longer glow in the dark because we stopped fellowshipping with the Light. We traded prayer for entertainment. We are too busy scrolling to open our Bibles. Slowly but surely we've lost our glow, and we haven't gotten it back because we no longer fellowship with the Light.

OUR SILENCE IS SPEAKING

Maybe the most concerning thing I see among those who are supposed to be saints of God is the fact that we are no longer bothered by the things that grieve the heart of God. If we truly love Jesus the way we claim we do, how can we ignore that which He weeps over? Living as a light in darkness means that we cannot sit idly by as a corrupt anti-Christ agenda marches forward unopposed. I know many reading this have probably thought to themselves, "I just don't want to offend anyone" or perhaps, "I would hate to hurt their feelings." Friend, it would be worth hurting their feelings temporarily if it keeps them from hell eternally. Someone has to shine in the darkness. We must speak up! By saying nothing, we are in fact saying something. We are saying that we will not stand against racial injustice. We are saying that we will not stand against those who are murdering the unborn. We are saying that we will not stand for the sanctity of marriage between one man and one woman. Our silence is saying much more than you think. If we choose to adapt to the culture around us and blend in as though nothing is happening, then that alone is a sign that we are no longer intimately connected to the Light. Anyone who lives in fellowship with the Light will shine in darkness. You are not called to live like the raven. You are called to stand like Elijah.

CHAPTER 9
OUTPOURINGS & ORANGE JUICE

I am about to share with you what may seem like one of the saddest verses in Elijah's story. If you are like me, it will at first make you really feel for the guy. Remember, this rugged prophet just kind of showed up out of nowhere and immediately displayed audacious courage by proclaiming a drought over corrupt Israel. Heaven must have cheered as this valiant vessel stood as a voice of righteousness.

From there God rolled out His master plan to feed Elijah by the ravens and to give him water from the brook Cherith. Like I've said before, you would think that in response to Elijah's bold obedience God would uphold him by much grander means. Of course, you know the story tells us otherwise. Then, in what seems like an attempt to just add insult to injury, scripture records something that seems so unfair. It says, *"And it happened after a while that the brook dried up, because there had been no rain in the land." (1 Kings 17:7)*

What a blow! Imagine how you would feel if you were Elijah. First, you were fed by a bunch of filthy ravens. Then, things went from bad to worse. Someone forgot to pay the water bill and now the brook Elijah had been drinking from is just a dusty old creek bed.

I'm not trying to question God's kindness—but man, I must say, He sure did not make this easy on Elijah. Couldn't He have just supernaturally supplied water to that individual brook the whole drought so His prophet would be sustained? Why give him the run-around,

...ing him go from place to place for provision?

The next couple of verses say, *"Then the word of the LORD came to him, saying, 'Arise, go to Zarephath, which belongs to Sidon, and dwell there. See, I have commanded a widow there to provide for you.'" (1 Kings 17:8-9)*

Here's my question. If the ravens and the brook were getting the job done, why send him to the widow? It just all seems a bit scattered and strange to me. I can't say for sure, but I have a pretty good guess as to what God was doing in this instance. I think God was putting all the necessary pieces in place to help ensure that Elijah would not start focusing on the wrong thing.

Let me explain. I believe God allowed the brook to dry up so that Elijah would keep his eyes on the Source rather than the system. God was making sure that Elijah did not do what we've all too often done. He was making sure that this prophet's eyes were on the Provider rather than the provision.

Are you seeing it? Let me ask you, what would you have done if you were in Elijah's shoes when the brook dried up? I can tell you what I would have done. I hate to admit it but since God used a brook the first time, I probably would have gone looking for another brook. In my limited thinking, I would have expected God to operate in the future the same way He chose to operate in the past. That is why God lets brooks dry up from time to time.

SUPERFICIAL SHACKLES

In my book *Jesus Isn't A Hipster*, there is a chapter where I share in great detail about the environment I was in when my life was radically turned upside down. The culture was very specific and uniquely different from what I had always been around growing up. We were at a youth conference, and for the first time in my teen years I had a head-on collision with the Holy Spirit. I was already part of an amazing church that was genuinely hungry for a move of God, but the aesthetics of my church were very different. There was something about getting away from my normal environment that helped open my eyes. Thankfully when I returned home, my church had a tremendous system in place to help with my spiritual growth.

Yet, I still got tripped up many times in the years that followed. I wasn't getting tripped up with compromise and complacency. I was getting tripped up by a very superficial mindset that I had subconsciously embraced. I somehow concluded that God would only *really* move in power among those who did church the same way they did church at the conference I had attended in my early teens. At that conference the band wasn't led by a little church sister on the Hammond B3 organ. It was led by a young, long haired, college kid with a scraggly beard and a screaming electric guitar. There were no stained-glass windows in the sanctuary. As a matter of fact there were no windows at all, just lots of fog and

LED lights.

It all seems so superficial now. But for years following that experience, I unknowingly tried to limit God to that moment. I made the faulty assumption of believing that God would regulate Himself to my preferred order of operation. Boy was I in for a rude awakening!

In the years that followed it was as though God decided to wage an all-out war against my limited mindset. I was privileged to travel with my father in the faith to churches and conferences that spread from one end of the spectrum to the other. Guess what I discovered? God moved just as powerfully in the backwoods of Alabama as He did in New York City. He moved in the suit-and-tie assemblies just as powerfully as He did in the congregations filled with those in skinny jeans and v-necks. Time after time God has shown me that He doesn't need the brook Cherith for His supernatural waters to flow. He can move through a lowly widow just as easily as He can through those filthy old ravens.

Whenever we demand that the Source fit within our systems, we run the risk of missing Heaven's intervention. Everything we need may well be right under our nose and we still miss it, simply because we are expecting it to come in our present through the same means that it came in our past. When we see a brook dry up in our lives it is really the mercy of God on display.

It is often His way of telling us to make sure we do not miss the Source, by becoming so focused on the system.

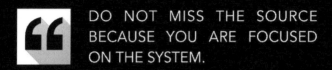

DO NOT MISS THE SOURCE BECAUSE YOU ARE FOCUSED ON THE SYSTEM.

BRANDING BLUNDERS

Let's talk about a breakfast staple—orange juice! Much more goes into crafting that glass of orange juice than the masses seeking it out may realize. Pulp or no pulp in this sweet and tart treat was the least important controversy one brand faced a few years back. Tropicana invested a whopping 35 million dollars into rebranding their classic, highly sought-after orange juice. After months of preparation, where they sank lots of time and money into creating a more compelling product design, the company officially launched their new look in January of 2009. Within a few months' time they were pulling the plug on their rebrand initiative. Sales had dropped by 20%, which resulted in an approximate loss of 30 million dollars. By the time you add up what the company had paid out to the advertising agency in charge of the rebrand, what they lost by the lack of sales following the re-launch, and all necessary steps taken to reinstate the old familiar look, and everything in between, Tropicana ended up with a loss of over 50 million dollars.[1] Ouch!

Pause for a minute and really think this through. This company lost 50 million dollars essentially due to the fact that customers went to stores looking for a specific product, which the stores actually had, yet missed it because it was in a package they were not expecting.

If there is anything I want you to catch from this chapter it's this: Outpourings and orange juice often come in packages you do not expect. What you are looking for could be right in front of you. Are you missing it because it is in a package you were not expecting? Dead men choose to throw their personal preferences and superficial desires aside. Regardless of how God decides to move, be it through a raven and a withering brook, or through the hands of a widow, it does not matter. They just want to be a part of whatever He is doing.

HEAVEN'S PERSPECTIVE

As we continue on this journey, I challenge you to ask the Lord to give you His perspective. Ask Him to help you see and remove any preconceived ideas that may be keeping you from what He desires to do in your life. The Church cannot afford to miss what God is doing in our present because He isn't doing it the way He did in our past. Whatever it looks like and whatever it sounds like, I just want to be in the middle of Heaven's operation.

CHAPTER 10
THE WORTH OF WINTER

A great general in the faith who has gone on to glory, Bishop Tony Miller, often said, "God is always preparing us for what He has prepared for us." If you look back over your life with eyes of discernment you will see that everything you have faced, and all that you have endured, have strategically been preparing you for this moment. Your future will prove that God was indeed very intentional with your past. In the years to come, I believe that if the Elijahs of the twenty-first century will take their place, we will watch as God takes some of the most unlikely candidates and turns them into some of the greatest champions of the gospel.

I believe we will watch rioters turn into revivalists. Those who have used their lives to spread hate will give their lives to spread hope. The ones who were once caught up in retaliation will be summoned for the emerging reformation. The most hopeless of sinners will be known as the most heroic of saints. I truly believe we are about to see a generation that the Church had written off, turn to God in radical repentance.

Yet before God does this miraculous work in our world there is something more He must do within us. Before we can address the great enemies of our society, we must first address the greatest enemy we are inwardly facing. This is where things can get uncomfortable for those who say yes to living the life of a dead man.

I can tell you, without hesitation, what I believe is the

most lethal threat facing modern American Christians. It is not war or famine. It's not a corrupt government or another pandemic. It's not even persecution. Friend, you and I are our own greatest threat. Without a divine turnaround, many of the Elijahs who are called to spearhead this battle will self-destruct. If we refuse the work Heaven wants to do in us, then we forfeit the work Heaven wants to do through us. Too many are on the brink of self-destruction. Our carnal appetite has caused us to become our own worst enemy. We are so obsessed with living in the lap of luxury that we are running the risk of forfeiting our very destiny.

Because of His great love, God has allowed the lives of His Elijahs to be shaken. A tsunami of His mercy has come to wage war on the earthly comforts that are lulling God's forerunners to sleep. You read that right. I called it mercy. It is in fact the mercy of God that has allowed us to be shaken from our slumber. Heaven is waging war on our man-made paradise. Because God has a mighty work *for* us, He must do a mighty work *in* us. Will you let Him have His way with your life? Heaven cannot use those who say yes to the call but no to the cutting. Before you can light a fire, you must be tried by fire.

Here is the crux of what I must communicate in this chapter. All who are called to lead in the coming revolution must pass through the Refiner's fire. There are no shortcuts or easy outs. If you want to be a part of

Heaven's plan you must embrace Heaven's process.

 IF YOU WANT TO BE A PART OF HEAVEN'S PLAN YOU MUST EMBRACE HEAVEN'S PROCESS.

A PLACE CALLED REFINEMENT

We have been exploring the life of this interesting character named Elijah. Now we are about to move to a new scene as he leaves the brook Cherith where the ravens have been feeding him, and heads to his next destination, Zarephath. At Zarephath, which actually means refinement[1] in the original language, Elijah faced one of his greatest challenges thus far. Here is what scripture says about the scene:

> *"Then the word of the LORD came to him, saying, 'Arise, go to Zarephath, which belongs to Sidon, and dwell there. See, I have commanded a widow there to provide for you.' So he arose and went to Zarephath. And when he came to the gate of the city, indeed a widow was there gathering sticks. And he called to her and said, 'Please bring me a little water in a cup, that I may drink.' And as she was going to get it, he called to her and said, 'Please bring me a morsel of bread in your hand.' So she said, 'As the LORD your God lives, I do not have bread, only a handful of flour in a bin, and a little oil in a jar; and see, I am*

> *gathering a couple of sticks that I may go in and prepare it for myself and my son, that we may eat it, and die.'" (1 Kings 17:8-12)*

Let me ask, which would be more difficult for you—to receive God's provision through some mangy ravens or to receive God's provision through some meager widow? I think I know the answer for most of those reading this book. You're like me. The ravens aren't exactly my preference, but I sure do not want to be known as the guy who took the last meal of a little widow at the end of her rope.

Or what about the widow? What if you were in her shoes? Imagine looking in the pantry and coming to the painstaking realization that you and your son only have enough food for one final meal and then, it's adios! Could you obey God when it made absolutely no sense?

Regardless of which character you feel more sympathetic towards, this scene makes one thing clear—God was not trying to make things easy for anyone. I hate to say it, but I think that is kind of the point. The Refiner's fire is all about pushing us beyond our preconceived limits. If you are Elijah, you are probably thinking there is no way you can ask a little widow to give up her last bite of food. If you are the widow, you are thinking there is no way you can let your son starve to death. So you must decide: Do I live within my limits, or do I trust God and press beyond my preconceived boundaries?

Let's do a little object lesson to drive the point home. I want you to raise your hand as high as you can. No seriously, lift a hand as high up into the air as possible and leave it lifted as you read on. Do you have it up? Keep it up! Now, with your hand still lifted as high as you can raise it, I want you to raise it a little higher. Come on just a little more. Did you do it?

After seeing this illustration many years ago at a conference I have since adopted it and illustrated this point dozens of times through the years. When you ask an audience to raise their hands as high as they can, then a few seconds later challenge them to raise them a little higher, nearly everyone in the room ends up going a few inches higher. Why? Because even when we think we are giving our all, the reality is we almost always have a little left that we have been holding back.

In the Kingdom, whatever we hold back, is actually holding us back. The Lord dropped a phrase in my spirit years ago that I have repeated hundreds of times now because it's simply true: It is not the 80% you are giving God that is killing you—it's the 20% you're holding onto.

This is why you must go through the Refiner's fire before you can lead a revolution. You cannot hold anything back. Once God brings you to a place where you fully trust Him, He wants to bring you to a place where He can fully trust you. That's why He sends us from the brook Cherith to a little widow in Zarephath.

WINTER IS WORTH IT

A while back Ali and I made what was probably the most exciting purchase of our married life. We were ecstatic, but we also felt a little lame. Let me explain. We were just a few short months away from our son's arrival and we had planned to have a little babymoon getaway. We didn't have a lot of extra money laying around, so we were thinking about just doing a nice, quiet, long weekend stay at a resort close to home. As the date approached however, we started to toy with another idea. It wasn't as romantic, nor was there anything overly spectacular about the idea. Yet the more thought we gave to it, the more excited we got about scratching the babymoon trip and putting those funds toward something much more resourceful—we bought a bed. I know, I know. This was the most adult decision of our lives! We asked each other several times, "Is this what getting old feels like? Are we really this excited about a bed?"

As much as I hate to admit it, cutting the babymoon trip and upgrading from a queen to a king size bed was probably one of the best decisions we have ever made! The only drawback during the entire process was the shopping experience. A bad car salesman pales in comparison to a bad bed salesman. For the record, you should know that for every bad salesman we encountered, we dealt with ten top notch salesmen. That being said, I honestly cannot communicate how obnoxious this one particular gentleman was. He was beyond pushy. He had no concern in knowing what we were looking for or how much we could spend. It was his way or the highway. Then, to make matters worse, this guy had the gift of gab like no one I have ever met. What should have been a twenty-minute visit turned into an hour long stay—and we did not find the bed we wanted.

Sorry, I didn't mean to vent. I have apparently had this bottled up for far too long! As frustrating as this part of our experience was, I did learn something very interesting. This salesman had just returned from a company seminar and was eager to share all of his newfound knowledge with whomever had a listening ear. In talking with him I discovered that their company, which has factories all across America, purchases almost all of their supplies locally. He said all of the padding, fabric, thread, things of that nature, come from the communities where they are located. However there is one product he told me they never even consider buying locally and that is wood.

This particular company buys all of their wood from Canada. When I asked him their reason for doing this he said, "It's because the trees in Canada have to endure a much harsher winter which makes them much stronger than what we have available here in the states." Being a preacher, naturally my ears perked up a bit when he shared this with me.

GROWING STRONGER

Friend, I want to encourage you as you journey through this time of refinement. Your winter season is not meant to destroy you. It is meant to strengthen you. Allow the Refiner to have His perfect work in your life and you will come out much stronger on the other side.

The story of this little widow goes on to say that when she obeyed the prophet Elijah in her season of testing and gave him all that she had left, God supernaturally replenished her supplies. She had provision throughout the entire duration of the drought. When we give God what's left, He gives us what's missing. In this winter season of refinement allow God to do His perfect work in you, so that He may do His perfect work through you.

CHAPTER 11
THE STORY DOESN'T END HERE

God has an interesting way of working in cycles. I'm not saying that we can box Him in and know His every move. We've already talked about the consequences of that tragic mistake. However, many times you will discover that what God did in the past He will do again in the future. For example, in Genesis, the very first book of the Bible, it says that God created the heavens and the earth. Then in Revelation, the very last book of the Bible, it says that John saw a new heaven and a new earth.

These fascinating parallels happen all through the Bible. While it is rare that God does the same thing the same way, He does indeed often give us a bit of a roadmap as to what He will do based upon what He has done. That is one reason there is such value in exploring these Old Testament stories.

In the last chapter we spent some time looking at Elijah and his relationship with the little widow from Zarephath. In this chapter I want us to draw some prophetic insights for our generation from one character we have not talked much about, the widow's son.

We're not given a ton of information about this young man. All we really know is that after we read about God supernaturally sustaining the widow's food supply, the Bible says,

> *"Now it happened after these things that the son of the woman who owned the house became sick. And his sickness was so serious*

that there was no breath left in him. So she said to Elijah, 'What have I to do with you, O man of God? Have you come to me to bring my sin to remembrance, and to kill my son?' And he said to her, 'Give me your son.' So he took him out of her arms and carried him to the upper room where he was staying, and laid him on his own bed." (1 Kings 17:17-19)

There you have it. All we know about this guy is that he is the son of a widow, which of course means he is fatherless, and that he had an untimely, premature death. We never really get a glimpse into much more of who this fellow is. His identity is buried far beneath the painful slate of cards that life dealt him and his family.

Are you seeing the parallel? Solomon wasn't kidding when he said that there is nothing new under the sun. There is an undeniable resemblance between the emerging generation of our day, and the widow's son. Life has handed both undeniable difficulties. We don't know much about who they are because of the immense pain they have experienced. They're both fatherless. And without an Elijah on the scene this generation will also die with an unfulfilled destiny.

WE NEED YOU

Let me bring you up to speed as to how serious this issue is. Around the year 2017 I wrote a very simple blog titled *Dad, we need you*. In that blog I shared some heart wrenching statistics about the fatherless generation that we are a part of. I have since shared this article every year on Father's Day to further shine light on this critical issue. Here is what I wrote:

"Dad, we need you.

We need you because 71% of young men and young women come from fatherless homes.

We need you because 90% of homeless and runaway children come from fatherless homes.

We need you because 85% of children with behavioral disorders come from fatherless homes.

We need you because 71% of teenage pregnancies happen among those who come from fatherless homes.

We need you because 85% of youth in prison come from fatherless homes.

We need you because 63% of those that commit suicide before age 18 come from fatherless homes.

We need you because 80% of those who abuse others sexually come from fatherless homes.

We need you because a child is four times more likely to grow up in poverty when they come from a fatherless home.

We need you because 24 million children, 1 out of 3, are living without you.[1,2]

Dad, we really need you."

The sad reality is that far too many are dying outside of their destiny because "dad" isn't in the picture. Acknowledging this fact is not meant to belittle the role that moms play in any way. I know some precious single mommas and I am telling you they are my heroes! On the flip side, we cannot underestimate the significance of a father and what all too often happens in their absence. What are we to do with this situation? How are the Elijahs of the twenty-first century going to respond?

Thankfully the widow's son's story does not end on his death bed. And if we will play our part, this generation's story does not have to be cut short either. Elijah refused to let the widow's son die prematurely. Heaven is looking for a company of Elijahs who will not allow this generation to die outside of their destiny!

WHEN I ACCIDENTALLY GOT ENGAGED

Have you ever heard of missionary dating? The term comes from the idea of dating someone who isn't a Christian with the intention of converting them to Christ. For the record, let me be very clear in stating that I have long denounced missionary dating. My wife and I even wrote a book called *The Rules of Romance Before Marriage* where we spend one chapter completely debunking the whole "flirt to convert" initiative.

Nevertheless, on my very first mission trip I went to the beautiful Guyana, South America and came back engaged — accidentally. I took missionary dating to a whole new level! Though Ali and I were not yet married, we were within months of our engagement when this happened.

Here's the story. I had the honor of traveling to Guyana with Pastor Keith Nix, a place he went on an annual basis and held crusades that would draw multiplied thousands. One night, after Pastor Keith had finished preaching a tremendous message where hundreds ran to the altar, we were waiting on our ministry hosts to pick us up. When they arrived, we climbed into the back of the car and I happened to be seated next to a very friendly Guyanese lady that looked to be around my age. She talked to me throughout the entire ride back to where we were staying. There was just one problem. Though they speak English, they have this beautiful Guyanese dialect that kept this ole country boy from understanding a lick of what they were saying.

I have never done well at understanding anything but backwoods, redneck, southern English. If I am in a service where someone with a distinct accent is preaching, I have to watch those I trust to know when to say amen because I can't understand a word of it. I don't mean to be offensive in the least bit. Unfortunately, to make my point I must bare my ignorance before the world!

So, as we were riding back to our quarters, with this little lady just talking away, I sat cordially smiling and nodding the whole time. At one point while she was talking I glanced over at Pastor Keith, and I knew something was wrong. It felt like he was staring holes through my soul. It was obvious that I was in some kind of deep trouble. Periodically I'd glance back at him and each time he would be staring at me with fire in his eyes. I was so nervous about going back to the room with him.

A few minutes before we arrived, while this young lady continued talking, I noticed out of the corner of my eye that Pastor Keith was laughing. I looked away for a moment to make certain, and then realized, he wasn't just laughing a little bit. He was cackling! I was so confused. The whole ride back he was staring holes through me and now he's belly laughing? I didn't know what in the world was going on.

When we finally got inside, he was still choked up with laughter. I had been many places with Pastor Keith; something was definitely up. He never acted like that. So I finally asked what on earth was going on and he told me, while still laughing, how he thought he was going to have to rebuke me. He said the whole way back she had been asking me questions about my love life—was I single, was I interested in dating, and so on. And the entire time I just sat there, grinning from ear to ear and shaking my head yes. I had practically pledged marriage to that girl! He was furious at my lack of character, until she asked me a question that demanded a specific response. When I just sat there and continued smiling and shaking my head like a goon, it dawned on him that I could not understand a word she was saying!

PUT YOURSELF IN THEIR PLACE

When I look at the relationship between the Church and this generation, who is like the widow's dead son, I feel like we are trying to have a conversation with a group that doesn't speak the same language. It's like me in the back of that car that night—we don't understand a word that is being said.

We see that they are bound in drugs and alcohol. We see that they are bound in pornography and sexual immorality. We see all of their hang-ups and bondages, yet we have been relatively ineffective in bringing change.

Why? Because you cannot understand what someone is trying to communicate until you understand where they are coming from. The Bible says that Elijah, *"Stretched himself out on the child three times, and cried out to the LORD and said, 'O LORD my God, I pray, let this child's soul come back to him.'" (1 Kings 17:21)*

> YOU CANNOT UNDERSTAND WHAT SOMEONE IS TRYING TO COMMUNICATE UNTIL YOU UNDERSTAND WHERE THEY ARE COMING FROM.

Until we put ourselves in the place of this dead generation, we will never be used of God to revive them.

We must stretch ourselves out over their broken condition, as Elijah did, until we know why they hurt the way they hurt. Far more than you may realize, their actions are in response to the dad that walked away, or the pain they have suffered, or the rejection they have felt. Their rebellion is their way of coping with the betrayal that they have had to endure. I'm not justifying their sin. I'm just telling you that until we understand what stole the life from them, we will never be able to revive them. Over and over in the gospels we see that some of Jesus's greatest miracles came after the Bible says that He was moved with compassion. Faith works by love. If we can't love a broken generation where they are, God cannot use us to raise them from their fatal state.

Loving the lost will cause your name to come into question at times. The religious crowd will never be comfortable with those God uses to revive a dead generation. Even Jesus was ridiculed for loving those dead in sin in a way that religion wasn't familiar with. They called Him a glutton and a winebibber. (See Luke 7:34) You can either bow to their godless demands and let this generation lay dead, or you can be a part of the Elijah company that raises them back to life.

QUIT PLAYING BY THE RULES

Interestingly, according to Numbers chapter nineteen, Elijah broke the rules when he stretched himself out over the dead boy. At that point, according to the law, the prophet was contaminated by the dead corpse. But you know how the story ends. Death didn't jump onto Elijah, life jumped onto the dead boy. The world needs what is within you, but they are never going to get it if you just live a mediocre life and play by the rules. Those who raise the dead are not intimidated by religious requirements. A fatherless generation desperately needs some Elijahs to stand up. They need to see a church that has quit playing by the rules of religion. They need someone who will fight for them to fulfill their destiny. God has some men and women who have died to selfish ambition, and they are about to step onto the battlefield. Let's go rescue a generation!

CHAPTER 12
REVEALING THEN REVIVAL

Before you can ever have a great revival, you must have a great revealing. Without a doubt, Heaven is laying bare the hearts of humanity in this hour. Sadly, we are seeing just as much scandal in the Church as we are in the world. Though times of exposure bring great turbulence, they are often the first rumblings of an emerging revival. Everyone acts like they want a move of God. However, few are willing to take off the blinders and come to a place where they understand—a move of God is not just a good idea, it's our only hope. Without a divine intervention our nation has passed the point of no return.

When the mantra of a country becomes one of corruption and compromise, it's a sign that Christians have bowed to culture. Our lamps have grown dim. The corruption we see in the world is a direct result of the compromise hiding in the Church. One of my heroes of the faith, the late revivalist Charles Finney, once said, "Brethren, our preaching will bear its legitimate fruits. If immorality prevails in the land, the fault is ours in a great degree. If there is a decay of conscience, the pulpit is responsible for it. If the public press lacks moral discrimination, the pulpit is responsible for it. If the Church is degenerate and worldly, the pulpit is responsible for it. If the world loses its interest in religion, the pulpit is responsible for it. If Satan rules in our halls of legislation, the pulpit is responsible for it. If our politics become so corrupt that the very foundations of our government are ready to fall away, the pulpit is responsible for it. Let us not ignore this fact, my dear brethren; but let us lay it to heart and be thoroughly awake to our responsibility in respect to the morals of this nation."[1]

It's as if Finney said these words while looking at the condition of the twenty-first century Church and its lack of impact in our society. Some have erroneously argued that the Church of America is brighter and more culturally relevant than ever before. We might have cultural relevance according to some, but what does it matter if we don't bring cultural change? If the Church of America is relevant on earth but unknown in Heaven, we have failed. If we are accepted by the world but rejected by God, we have fallen short. With such moral decay, what are we to do? How will Heaven respond? In times of deep darkness God raises up those who have been tried by fire — His Elijahs.

Once God puts us through the crucible of refinement and brings us to a place where we see the world around us the way that He sees it, He then sends us packing yet again. This time it's not to the lowly widow, it is to the corrupt king.

A DIVINE COLLISION

In 1 Kings chapter eighteen, in obedience to the Word of the Lord, Elijah went to appear before Israel's wicked king, Ahab. On his way he ran into Ahab's palace administrator, Obadiah, who the Bible refers to as a devout man of God. Elijah told Obadiah to go and let Ahab know that he had arrived. Obadiah began scrambling at Elijah's request! He told Elijah how furious Ahab had become after searching for him far and wide with no luck. Then Obadiah said to Elijah, *"And now you say, 'Go, tell your master, "Elijah is here"'! And it shall come to pass, as soon as I am gone from you, that the Spirit of the LORD will carry you to a place I do not know; so when I go and tell Ahab, and he cannot find you, he will kill me." (1 Kings 18:11-12)*

Nevertheless, once Elijah assured Obadiah that he was going to meet with Ahab that very day, Obadiah went to give the king the news. When Ahab saw Elijah, whom the king referred to as the troubler of Israel, Elijah called for a showdown of epic proportions.

The rugged prophet was standing on the cusp of a divine collision where Heaven and earth were about to forcefully intersect. Oftentimes when God chooses to confront the wickedness of humanity, He calls His remnant out of hiding and puts them center stage. This crew rarely fits within the religious confines of their day. They are of a different breed. They are those who refuse to go down without a fight. They are men and women who are not scared of anything because they have already died.

When Elijah irrupted from the shadows, he called for a showdown between light and darkness. Heaven has summoned you out of hiding to do the same. At Elijah's word, Ahab gathered all of Israel and the false prophets together at Mount Carmel. Breaking through the atmosphere of compromise like a voice of thunder, Elijah declared, *"How long will you falter between two opinions? If the LORD is God, follow Him; but if Baal, follow him." (1 Kings 18:21)*

In this moment, one man stood between Heaven and earth as a voice declaring enough is enough. He wasn't surrounded by an entourage of those who were on his side. As a matter of fact, it looked like he was outnumbered. But if God is on your side, no matter how many enemies stand before you, you are always the majority. Are there any Elijahs today who will stand up to address the compromise that is running rampant in the Church? Is there anyone who will raise their voice and declare that you cannot serve two masters? The divide between who we are in the light and who we are in the dark is sadly continuing to grow with each new day. We cannot change what is happening in the world until we change what is happening in the Church. We have become experts at performing. However, God is not judging us based upon what is happening on the stage as much as what is happening behind the scenes.

EVEN IN THE DARK IT COUNTS

A few years into our marriage I had boarded yet another dieting fad. Thank God for such a precious wife. Ali has always been so supportive of me—even if she secretly loathes my latest harebrained dieting idea! A couple of ways she has so graciously shown her support with each new diet I've participated in is by joining me in it and by preparing meals that accommodate the changes we have made. I really have it made with this girl!

After we had taken the plunge and started with these new eating habits during one particular diet, Ali was doing amazing. Her energy level was up to the point that she practically cut out all caffeine. She was experiencing great results. I on the other hand was not doing so well . . . I needed more coffee and, believe it or not, I actually gained weight. How does that even happen? Well in my case I can tell you exactly why I wasn't seeing results—I got caught red-handed.

One day while we were doing some chores around the house, I found an unopened box of brown sugar cinnamon pop tarts hidden hidden behind some of our other snacks. We must have bought them before we started the diet and forgot about them once we stashed them in the back of the pantry. That night, I'm sure it was the devil himself that came into my room to tempt me. I laid in bed for hours just thinking about those pop tarts. After Ali was sound asleep, I couldn't take it any longer. I tiptoed into the kitchen, opened the box, and dug in. Upon finishing, I hid the evidence and tucked the box back deep in the pantry. I kept this up for about a week – until one night I got caught.

I had just pulled a pop tart out and taken my first bite when I heard a voice from behind me say, "Caleb Pierce, what are you eating?" That was it. No hiding it. Time to confess. I turned around with a sly grin hoping to charm my way out of the situation and said, "You want a bite?" as I extended the pop tart to Ali. Annoyed, she said, "No wonder you aren't seeing results! How long have you been doing this?" Embarrassed I said, "About a week." Then she said, "Are you not going to take this serious? You're never going to see change if you do this kind of stuff!" Still trying to save face, I gave Ali a big grin and said, "I just thought if no one saw me, the calories wouldn't count."

Needless to say I learned my lesson that night! However, that's not the only lesson I learned from that situation. More importantly I learned that it is our compromise in the dark that is keeping us from change in the light. If you diet in the day but feast all night, for every two steps you take forward, you are taking twice as many steps back. I am afraid this mindset is at the heart of what Elijah was addressing in Israel. Too often God's people fall into the trap of trying to serve Him and the false gods of our culture simultaneously. When people lived like that in the old Church they would say, "If you try to keep one foot in the world and one foot in the Kingdom you will get torn in two." God is raising up a holy remnant who will confront this issue of compromise. He doesn't want us missing our opportunity in the light because of what we have tolerated in the dark.

WHEN FIRE FALLS

You probably know how this scene from Elijah's story

ends. He rolled out Heaven's divine strategy before the people, saying about the false prophets of Baal,

> *"Let them give us two bulls; and let them choose one bull for themselves, cut it in pieces, and lay it on the wood, but put no fire under it; and I will prepare the other bull, and lay it on the wood, but put no fire under it. Then you call on the name of your gods, and I will call on the name of the LORD; and the God who answers by fire, He is God." (1 Kings 18:23-24)*

After hours and hours of the false prophets cutting themselves and calling upon the name of Baal to respond with fire, Elijah called the people near as he prepared for God to show Himself strong. He built the altar and prepared the sacrifice, then gave this instruction to the people, *"Fill four waterpots with water, and pour it on the burnt sacrifice and on the wood." (1 Kings 18:33)* Three times he had them do this until everything was completely drenched. Then the prophet prayed and asked God to show that He was the only true God by consuming the sacrifice with fire. Sure enough fire fell and consumed everything! Elijah called for all of the false prophets of Baal to be executed, letting none of them escape. God honored the bold obedience of His obscure prophet by pouring out fire. Beloved, I believe we are about to see Him respond with fire once more.

NO EASY ROUTE

If the fire is going to fall on America again then we must return to the altar. We have to quit looking for the easy route. We have to put politically correct Christianity that never confronts, never challenges, and never changes anyone, in its grave once and for all. It may look like we are outnumbered, and like our altar has been drenched in water. Nevertheless, if God can find a company of Elijahs who will stand as an unwavering force of opposition to the corruption and compromise at work in our nation, He will respond with the fires of revival and awakening.

> WE HAVE TO PUT POLITICALLY CORRECT CHRISTIANITY THAT NEVER CONFRONTS, NEVER CHALLENGES, AND NEVER CHANGES ANYONE, IN ITS GRAVE ONCE AND FOR ALL.

Who is there that will refuse to stand for a church that falters between God and cultural idols? Who will stand in opposition to the idea that we can be one person in private and another in public? Are there any Elijahs who will quit trying to avoid confrontation, come back to the altar, and let God respond with fire? It's time to come out of hiding. Heaven is watching and earth is waiting for you to take your place.

CHAPTER 13

KEEP SOWING

Some of the most famous and provocative words ever uttered by the fearless Scottish reformer, John Knox, must be, "Give me Scotland or I'll die."[1] These six simple words revealed the endless depth of Knox's commitment to see cultural transformation no matter the cost. Our society is in desperate need of men and women of such caliber. Does this degree of relentless determination still exist? Where are those with such tenacious faith? The American Church has become anemic and powerless in the arena of perseverance. It seems that our faith falters every time the wind blows. Yet, Jesus said, *"No one, having put his hand to the plow, and looking back, is fit for the kingdom of God." (Luke 9:62)* The "feelings-based" gospel so many have built their lives upon has left them deprived of strength.

Because unwavering faith has become such a rare commodity, brokenness abounds. Hell's agenda runs rampant in our nation with little opposition from the Church, because so few are left who have not bowed their knee to political correctness. Rather than standing against the onslaught of immortality, we simply allow the rising tide of corruption to carry us wherever it wishes. Our commitment to the cause of the gospel has become so fickle that we simply conform to whatever climate we are in.

God so detests this mentality that in Revelation 3:16 He says, *"Because you are lukewarm, and neither cold nor hot, I will vomit you out of My mouth."* Nevertheless,

God's track record shows that He has a plan for times such as these. When passivity becomes the default characteristic of the Church, Heaven raises up those of a different spirit, a people of passion and fire. Their very presence draws a line in the sand between the committed and the cowardly. This new breed has been sent from Heaven to separate those who will persist until what has been broken is fixed from those who do not want to deal with the inconvenience of brokenness.

A NEW ERA, A NEW ERROR

I grew up in the era of VCRs. Our television had metal rabbit ears coming out of the back of it. We did not have cable, so if you wanted to change the channel, out of the handful of options that we had, there was no such thing as a remote. You had to stand up, walk across the room, and turn a knob. How did we survive such perilous times? My brother and I got in trouble through the years for breaking the metal antennas off the TV and using them in sword fights. Rather than going and buying a new TV, do you know what we would do? My dad would rig up a coat hanger and aluminum foil in its place.

In my childhood when something broke, I watched countless times as my parents would tinker with it until it was fixed. We don't do that anymore. In this day and age when something is broken we don't fix it, we give up on it and get a new one. I wish that I was solely talking about things like TVs and household items.

Sadly, we have adopted this same mindset in nearly every area of life. A new era brought about a new error. It seemed as though everyone in my grandparent's generation had marriages that lasted half a century, even unto death. When their marriages were broken, they fixed them. Today when marriages are broken, we just give up and get a new one. Many of our grandparents would spend their entire adult career at one job. Today people change jobs about as often as they change clothes. Previous generations would faithfully serve in the same church all their lives. When things were broken, they stayed the course and helped right the ship. Not anymore. If we don't like something that's going on, we just find somewhere else to go.

I think this trend reveals a tragically sad reality. We are the generation that gives up on broken things. When you consider the purpose of the gospel, this is devastating. In Luke chapter four when Jesus came to the synagogue in Nazareth and stood up to teach, of all the places He could have chosen to read from, the Bible says that He purposefully found one particular passage from Isaiah 61 that says these words,

> *"The Spirit of the Lord is upon Me, because He has anointed Me to preach the gospel to the poor; He has sent Me to heal the brokenhearted, to proclaim liberty to the captives and recovery of sight to the blind, to set at liberty those who are oppressed; To proclaim the acceptable year*

of the Lord." (Luke 4:18-19)

This reveals a paramount truth that we dare not miss. Jesus is a coat hanger and aluminum foil kind of God. He doesn't give up on broken things and throw them to the curb. Let's not kid ourselves. Giving up on that which is broken is much easier than dragging it to the workshop. Tending to what seems to be working is much more convenient than catering to that which is messed up. Sadly, that is exactly what we have done in the American Church. There is nothing costly about having weekly church services where we sit in a nice, padded chair in our state-of-the-art auditoriums, listening to world-class orators and five-star bands. Though none of us want to admit it, the reality is that the entire design of the modern American Church is built to repel the broken and appease the comfortable.

God is looking for people of persistence. His eyes are scouring the earth for those who will be a part of the Isaiah 61 company. He is assembling a holy remnant that will not give up on a broken generation—an army of dead men who refuse to let the world around them die outside of their God-given destiny. I believe we are ripe for a divine disruption. Though things look dark, we are in the perfect position for Heaven to invade earth. There is a remnant who will not settle for the status quo. They will not give up on that which is broken because they know Heaven has a plan for this generation that has yet to be fulfilled.

DOGGED DETERMINATION

Few characters in the Bible better exemplify dogged determination than Elijah. After the Mt. Carmel victory where God poured out fire, Elijah went to Ahab, probably in a bloody mess having just slaughtered the prophets of Baal, and told him to prepare for rain because the drought was about to end. Ahab did as Elijah directed and the Bible says,

> *"Elijah went up to the top of Carmel; then he bowed down on the ground, and put his face between his knees, and said to his servant, 'Go up now, look toward the sea.' So he went up and looked, and said, 'There is nothing.' And seven times he said, 'Go again.' Then it came to pass the seventh time, that he said, 'There is a cloud, as small as a man's hand, rising out of the sea!' So he said, 'Go up, say to Ahab, "Prepare your chariot, and go down before the rain stops you."' Now it happened in the meantime that the sky became black with clouds and wind, and there was a heavy rain."*
> (1 Kings 18:42-45)

What was Elijah doing? Why did he keep sending his servant to look toward the sea for rain? If you grew up in a household that was anything like the one I grew up in then you should know exactly what Elijah was doing. I can't count the number of times I had my backside blistered for arguing with my parents over cleaning my room. They would tell me to go straighten up and I would start rattling off a million excuses to get out of it. Every time they would respond by saying, "I am not taking no for an answer! Go clean your room!"

Every time Elijah was told that his servant did not see any rain clouds, he sent him to look again because he would not take no for an answer. What he saw in the natural did not line up with what he saw in the spirit, and he refused to settle in defeat when he knew God had plans that had not yet come to pass.

If ever there has been an hour that we need people with Elijah's depth of determination, who will persist until they prevail, it is now. Our generation may be broken, and it may seem as though all hope is lost, but for those who have an ear to hear what the Spirit is saying to the Church we know that it is far from over. This generation will be saved! God has a remnant of Elijahs who will not settle for anything other than an undeniable awakening.

> WE MUST PERSIST UNTIL WE PREVAIL!

Is this generation free from sin and compromise? Look again! Have the chains of sexual promiscuity been broken? Look again! Have they surrendered their all to Jesus? Look again! We will not take no for an answer.

Even in this present drought we know that rain is coming.

PLANT THE SEED

Some of my favorite New Testament verses say, *"Elijah was a man with a nature like ours, and he prayed earnestly that it would not rain; and it did not rain on the land for three years and six months. And he prayed again, and the heaven gave rain, and the earth produced its fruit." (James 5:17-18)* Many scholars agree that by this point the drought would have taken such a toll on Israel that they were most likely being sustained by other nations. They were living at the mercy of the world around them—that's another message for another time. This drought was no joke! But did you catch what verse 18 said? It said that when it started raining, the earth began producing fruit. You mean to tell me that after a drought of three and a half years the earth was fruitful? That can only mean one thing. Someone was sowing seed even during the drought.

To every Elijah who feels like throwing in the towel; to everyone who has assessed the damage and feels like this generation is too far gone; to all who feel like an awakening is nothing more than a far-fetched dream, I want to encourage you! Keep sowing seed. I know at times it feels like we've gone three and a half years without a drop of rain. However, if we refuse to settle for brokenness and continue sowing even in drought, we can rest assured that one day soon God is going to pour out the rains of revival and we are going to see a harvest.

CHAPTER 14
UNITED FORCE

Every hero faces hard seasons. Joseph faced the pit and prison. Moses faced the Red Sea. David faced Goliath. Daniel faced the lion's den. There are endless examples found throughout both the Old and New Testament—and that is kind of the point. God wanted to make sure that we always have a blueprint to follow in difficult seasons. Possibly the most famous chapter in the Bible, Psalm 23, has been etched on our hearts because at some point we must all face that which seems like the valley of the shadow of death. No one is exempt. Anyone that lives long enough will experience the dark night of the soul. The question is not, will I face difficulties? The question is *how* will I face difficulties?

Elijah was no stranger to this reality. You can either make the mistakes others have made or you can learn from the mistakes others have made. After the Mt. Carmel victory Elijah made a glaring mistake. When Ahab told Jezebel about Elijah's victory and how he took a sword and slaughtered all the false prophets, she was infuriated. She sent word to Elijah saying, *"So let the gods do to me, and more also, if I do not make your life as the life of one of them by tomorrow about this time." (1 Kings 19:2)*

This message floored Elijah. When he heard Jezebel's plans, the Bible says that he ran for his life! First, he went to Beersheba, where he left his servant. Then he went on by himself into the wildernesses, laid under a tree, and started begging God to take his life.

SCARED SENSELESS

Is it just me or does this part of Elijah's story make your head spin? Within just a few short verses he went from being God's man of great faith and power, to being a man that was scared senseless. He literally went from one extreme to the other. How does this happen?

I am not here to criticize Elijah. I could have made the same mistakes he made just as easily had I been in his shoes. Yet I believe if we look closely at how he got into this predicament we can avoid going down the same path. Why did the same man that had just called fire down from Heaven and prayed until the flood gates of Heaven were opened, go running for his life after a wicked queen said she was coming after him? Surely if he had the courage to take on the false prophets, he had the courage to take on Jezebel! Elijah must have ran because he failed to realize one important revelation: we are most vulnerable after victory.

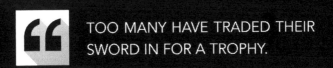

TOO MANY HAVE TRADED THEIR SWORD IN FOR A TROPHY.

I too have made this mistake more times than I care to count. Success often leads to susceptibility. We conquer what must be conquered and then we start to coast. That's where we get in trouble. We start letting our guard down. As we step into a new battle, we find ourselves vulnerable because we've traded our sword in for a trophy.

WHAT ARE YOU DOING HERE?

Feeling defeated, this once fearless prophet found some shade under a tree and put himself to sleep asking God to end his life. Two times while he laid there feeling depressed and hopeless an angel awoke him with bread and water. The second time he was awakened the angel told him to eat and drink to replenish his strength for the journey ahead. Obeying the angel's command, Elijah ate and began a forty-day journey to Mt. Horeb.

Once he arrived the Bible says, *"And there he went into a cave, and spent the night in that place; and behold, the word of the LORD came to him, and He said to him, 'What are you doing here, Elijah?'" (1 Kings 19:9)*

Have you ever gotten in such a mess and veered so far off track that you felt like God was calling your name to ask you that same question, "What are you doing here?" God continued speaking to Elijah:

> *"'Go out, and stand on the mountain before the LORD.' And behold, the LORD passed by, and a great and strong wind tore into the mountains and broke the rocks in pieces before the LORD, but the LORD was not in the wind; and after the wind an earthquake, but the LORD was not in the earthquake; and after the earthquake a fire, but the LORD was not in the fire; and after*

the fire a still small voice. So it was, when Elijah heard it, that he wrapped his face in his mantle and went out and stood in the entrance of the cave. Suddenly a voice came to him, and said, 'What are you doing here, Elijah?'" (1 Kings 19:11-13)

God wasn't going to let Elijah off the hook. He had gotten himself in a bind, yet God loved him too much to let him stay in that position. Elijah had to recognize what led him to such a place of despair and brokenness. As God continued pressing him, "What are you doing here, Elijah?" he finally responded by saying that he believed he was the only true servant of the Lord that was left. And that's where God drew the line.

He told the prophet to go anoint three individuals, one of which was Elijah's replacement. The climatic verse in God's response to Elijah's bogus claim of being the only faithful follower left was when the Lord said, *"I have reserved seven thousand in Israel, all whose knees have not bowed to Baal, and every mouth that has not kissed him." (1 Kings 19:18)*

God was making it clear to Elijah that he had become quite delirious. If we don't respond correctly, times of difficulty will lead to times of delusion. It is when we are backed into a corner that our vision runs the greatest risk of becoming distorted. If we respond like Elijah did, we will make the mistake of believing that we are all alone when in reality God has seven thousand others who are still in the fight. Elijah wasn't just wrong. He was wrong by a long shot. How did he get so far off track? I believe it all traces back to verse three. When he heard Jezebel's plans the Bible says that he, *"...went to Beersheba, which belongs to Judah, and left his servant there." (1 Kings 19:3)*

Elijah got in trouble when he gave into isolation. We were never meant to take this journey alone. Friend, even those who win on the mountain top need others that they can lean on. Community is the cure for all ailments that come from isolation. In reality, all Elijah really needed was a friend who would look him in the eyes and tell him that he was not thinking straight. When we decide to take the journey alone, we set ourselves up for defeat.

STAY IN THE BODY

When Ali was about five months pregnant with Judah, I caught the worst cold I have ever had in my life. I don't want to be too graphic so let me just say that every time I blew my nose and tossed the tissues in the wastebasket, those tissues would be glowing in the dark! That might be stretching it a bit perhaps, but I am telling you, I was as sick as a dog. The greatest difficulty I had to deal with in fighting that cold, however, was not the physical aspect of what I faced but rather the mental challenge.

All I could think about was my son. I'm by no means a physician and I didn't have the first clue as to how viruses operate, but I was haunted by the possibility of

Ali catching the cold and passing it onto Judah in the womb. She was only five months pregnant—he was tiny! If he somehow contracted what I had, how could he possibly fight it off? My mind was racing a million miles a minute. So, as a Spirit filled man of God, full of mountain-moving faith, I did exactly what any other man of God would have done . . . I googled all my symptoms! My research put me in a bit of a perplexing position — a "good-news, bad-news" kind of situation. Let's start with the bad. Based upon all my research, checking off symptom after symptom, one thing was clear . . . I was about to die. Yep, I was apparently coming to the end. The tint of my mucus, the swelling in my throat, and the busting headache I had been dealing with all pointed to the most fatal disease found on the web. That's the bad news. Thankfully, against all odds, I survived! Now for the good news. Judah was going to be just fine. I am sure there is a more technical way to explain this, but all the medical jargon is way over my head. So here is my overly simplistic way of explaining it. Because my little boy was in Ali's womb, he did not have to depend solely on his ability to fight off sickness. He was covered by his mama's immune system. Because he was a part of her, her strength became his strength, and he did not have to rely on his own abilities. This made the likelihood of him catching anything serious very unlikely.

Why does the enemy work so hard to get you isolated and away from the Body of Christ? Because as long as you are in the body, you do not have to rely on your own strength. It is when we get alone, like Elijah leaving his servant and going on by himself, that we respond to difficulties incorrectly and end up in trouble. If there is any temptation those who walk in the spirit of Elijah face, it is the temptation of isolation.

A VULNERABLE POSITION

How are you doing in this area? Are you a part of a community of believers? Is your life intertwined with others who are also pursing God? If not, it's time to get honest with yourself and acknowledge that you have put yourself in an incredibly vulnerable position. That was why, when God spoke to Elijah on the mountain, He repeatedly asked him, "Why are you here?" God wasn't asking because He didn't know. He was asking to make sure Elijah knew. He was never meant to face the challenges he was facing alone.

If we are going to take on the powers of darkness that are wreaking havoc upon our nation, we must understand that we cannot do it alone. We must be a united force. Then, no matter what difficulties we may face, even if we lose our individual footing for a moment, we are surrounded by those who will pick us back up. Elijah, don't take another step by yourself. This journey was meant to be traveled with a family of believers.

CHAPTER 15
STAY THE COURSE

All my life it seems I have had soul winning bubbling up from deep inside of me. It's just in the reservoirs of my heart. As a kid, the desire to see others surrender their all to Christ wasn't something I had asked for. It was just there. It was a deposit God purposed for me to carry before I ever took my first breath. I have never been able to just sit back and ignore sin. Something inside of me demands that I take action and point the world around me to Jesus.

As I grew up, I started to understand the necessity of stewarding this deep conviction. Through the years I have consistently sought to grow in understanding and develop my ability to share the gospel with others. I've by no means arrived. Not even close! So please don't misunderstand what I'm about to say. Though I may not be where I want to be just yet, I must tell you I'm sure not where I was! To say that I have some real doozies in my rearview mirror would probably be the understatement of the century.

WHERE IT ALL BEGAN

My earliest memory of seeking to point a sinner to the Lord dates back to when I was around five years old. The neighbors that lived across the street from us had a son that was around my age and we became good pals. If he wasn't at our house, I was over at his. We were practically inseparable. As a kid I noticed that this family wasn't living right, especially the mom. I started planning in my mind how I could win her to Christ and came up with what seemed like an effective strategy at the time. While she was outside doing some yard work, I went out into the middle of our fairly busy neighborhood street and laid down with my arms stretched out wide, as though I were on a cross. Of course, as soon as she saw me she came running to my rescue screaming, "Caleb, get out of the road!" Laying there I began shouting back, "My name is not Caleb!" Since there were no cars coming from either direction she said, "Then who are you?" and I responded by saying something like, "My name is Jesus and I died for you. Repent and live for me." My act of lunacy actually worked! Once she got me off the street, she called my mom crying and asked her to pray with her.

I was hooked! Around the same age when I started school, my brother and I got in a fist fight on the bus one day on the way home. He was sitting with some of his friends, within earshot of where I was seated. He didn't realize that I was eavesdropping on their conversation. A few minutes into their chatter I heard several of his friends cussing up a storm. Being the kid evangelist that I was, I couldn't just sit idly by and ignore such foul language. I stood up in my seat and repeatedly shouted as loud as I could, "Repent or you're going to hell!" My brother, embarrassed, jumped up and charged toward me throwing punches left and right. While I had him coming at me from one angle, I had the bus driver screaming from behind the steering wheel, "Caleb, sit your behind down right now!" Sheesh, talk about warfare!

As embarrassing as some of these memories are they pale in comparison to the evangelistic escapades of my early teen years. For example, at one point my youth group had been learning about hearing and obeying the voice of God. So, one day while at the grocery store, I went down the sweets aisle and passed by a middle-aged man that was out doing his shopping. A thought crossed my mind that I mistakenly assumed was the Lord. This fella did not look like he was in the best of health. To say he was a heavier man is putting it nicely, and he had very labored breathing. As I watched him load down his cart, one thought kept resonating in my head that I assumed was from the Lord—heart attack. With knocking knees I worked up the courage to approach this gentleman and said, "Sir, I know this may sound strange, but as I passed by, I felt like God was speaking to me about you. I kept hearing the words *heart attack* each time I looked at you." As you can imagine his eyes got real wide and I continued, "Have you ever had a heart attack?" With a look of sheer terror on his face he shook his head no. Now listen, everything I had done up until this point was awful but let me assure you . . . I was just getting started. I looked him square in the eyes and said, "Well you're probably about to have one, but God wants to heal you and save you. Do you want to surrender to Jesus?" I cannot believe I did this! He didn't even respond. He just darted away as fast as he could.

Among all those I have tried to reach through the years, few have had to endure what my childhood friends endured as I sought to grow and mature in this gift. While I was the mastermind behind most of these erroneous tactics, I had one friend, my best friend to this day, that faithfully joined me in attempting to win our friends to the Lord. We would invite them over for sleepovers where we would lecture them on their sinful ways and then make an altar call. If that didn't work, we played the most gruesome scenes we could find from *The Passion Of The Christ* and tried to guilt them into surrender. And when all else failed we got on the internet and found videos shared by those who had supposedly drilled miles deep into the earth, sent down a microphone, and captured the screams of those burning in hell. If we couldn't convince them, and we couldn't guilt them, our only option left was to scare them into following Jesus!

I'm just scratching the surface with these stories. As you can see, when I say that God has brought me a long way, I'm not exaggerating. As whacky as my antics have been at various points during my life, there are very few things I treasure as much as joining someone as they begin their journey with Christ. While I cannot overstate how blessed I am by watching different ones I've walked with over the years succeed as they stay the course, I can't ignore the painstaking reality of how many I have watched set their hand to the plow and turn back only a few steps into their journey.

FEW STAY THE COURSE

I used to beat myself up over how many people I have watched turn their back on a life of radically pursuing Jesus over the years. I thought I was surely doing something wrong. Then I started talking to others who were serious about making disciples and realized that my experiences were really not all that unique. They too had witnessed the same pattern — only a few who begin the journey stay the course.

> FEW WHO BEGIN THE JOURNEY STAY THE COURSE.

Though this should grieve us, it really should not surprise us. When Jesus taught the parable of the sower in Matthew 13, He told us about four types of people and only one out of the four types was ultimately fruitful. When you read the text carefully you realize that the issue was not with the seed, it was with the soil. According to this parable, no matter how good your seed is or how well you communicate the message of the Kingdom, at best, you have about a 25% chance of success.

I think one of the most detrimental turning points in

the moral decline of our nation stems from this very issue. Over the years I am sure more ministers than we could imagine have been discouraged as they've watched so many turn away after saying they were all in. They had to decide how they would respond to the heartache. Would they remain faithful to the message of the Kingdom, or would they lower the bar so that no one felt uncomfortable by their lack of fruitfulness? Sadly, many chose the latter rather than the former. While we focused on getting people to sign a card, we quit caring about whether or not they ever bore any fruit. Who cares if they really live the life as long as they attend our church? This tragic choice has led our nation to a place of dire consequence.

MARCHING FORWARD

We weren't designed for retraction. The engine churning beneath the surface of our skin was only designed to move one direction — forward. Heaven will not tolerate a halfhearted commitment, in one day and out the next. Understanding how vile backtracking really is in the eyes of God, Solomon spared us of pristine speech and went straight for the jugular when he spoke on this matter saying, *"As a dog returns to his vomit, so a fool returns to his folly." (Proverbs 26:11 AMPC)* Nothing is more devastating than witnessing someone betray their commitment to Christ. While seeing someone turn away from Christ is absolutely heartbreaking, seeing someone turn away from the mission to which God has called them to is a pretty close second. When we forfeit our assignment, the very reason we are alive for this particular hour, it not only costs us, it costs all those we have been called to reach.

Friend, I don't want you to forfeit your destiny. I don't want you to miss the divine moment we are living in. Starting this journey isn't really the hard part. Staying the course is where the rubber meets the road.

The man that God called as Elijah's replacement must have known this. Whenever Elijah came down from the mountain, after running from Jezebel, he found Elisha plowing with his oxen. When Elijah got to Elisha, he threw his mantle on him, as to call him under his tutelage. The passage where this takes place ends by saying something somewhat bizarre. It says, *"So Elisha returned to his oxen and slaughtered them. He used the wood from the plow to build a fire to roast their flesh. He passed around the meat to the townspeople, and they all ate. Then he went with Elijah as his assistant." (1 Kings 19:21 NLT)*

Seems like a bit of a strange response if you ask me. Why wouldn't Elisha simply leave the oxen and follow after Elijah? I believe the way Elisha responded reveals the reason he was able to steward his calling so well. It also shows why he didn't do what so many in our generation do—eventually turn back. When he slaughtered his oxen and burned his plow, he was making sure that he had nothing in his past that could pull him away from where God was leading him. He made certain there was nothing to go back to.

BURNING BRIDGES

Every individual that has started to follow after Christ only to turn back, did so because they had oxen they refused to slaughter. Your oxen may be a career or an unhealthy relationship. Whatever it is, saying yes to the life of a dead man means that we lay everything that has ever competed for our affection at the feet of Jesus. Plowing with oxen isn't evil. In an agricultural society it was just a normal way of living. The greatest enemy to your destiny is normalcy. It is the number one reason people turn back. If you are going to catch the mantle and stay the course, you're going to have to make sure that you leave no bridges back to your former life of mediocrity. Heaven is calling you to a new degree of consecration.

CHAPTER 16
A FAMILY FEUD

Whenever Elijah threw his mantle on Elisha it marked the initiation of a new day. The transfer of power had begun. Soon enough Elisha would rise in the spirit of Elijah, standing as an unrelenting force from Heaven. Nevertheless, Elijah wasn't going to go out quietly. His remaining days as Israel's premier prophet were marked with more quarrels between him and the corrupt king and queen. As if the wicked legacy they had been establishing wasn't enough, Ahab and Jezebel plunged even further into injustice by having an innocent man named Naboth murdered so they could take his vineyard. As you would imagine, Elijah continued to stand boldly against their treacherous acts. This prophet of holy fury refused to turn a blind eye to such injustice. Surely, as you evaluate the depravity that is feverishly at work in our society, you understand why God is raising up men and women who will say *yes* to Heaven's mandate just as Elijah did. With unmatched conviction, his heart would not allow him to tolerate the sin that was running rampant in Israel.

To be clear, Elijah wasn't just going around picking fights with Ahab and Jezebel because he had some personal vendetta with them. His issue was with sin. The sins of Israel had caused this nation, chosen by God, to enter one of her darkest days. Elijah was raised up as a voice to wage war against anything that sought to take Israel away from her God-given purpose.

1 Kings ends by telling us that Ahab died and the dogs

A FAMILY FEUD

licked his blood just as the Lord had said. Unfortunately, Ahab's death did not mark the end of Israel's iniquity. Elijah continued his feud with the king's successor, Ahaziah, the son of Ahab.

Elijah completely and utterly detested Ahaziah because he chose to follow in the footsteps of his corrupt father. To fully understand how extreme Elijah's intolerance of sin really was, you have to read 2 Kings 1. Spoiler alert, here is what happened: Three times Israel's new, corrupt, commander-in-chief sent an entourage to seize Elijah and bring him back. In response, two of the three times Elijah called fire down upon the king's servants killing them all. Finally, when the third group arrived and the captain of the group begged Elijah to spare them, Elijah went with them back to the king and pronounced a death sentence over him. Sure enough, the chapter ends with Ahaziah's death.

So what's the moral of the story? Elijah was not playing any games. He simply refused to oblige Ahaziah and return with his servants until an angel spoke to him and told him to do so. Yet, in my opinion, it seems as though Elijah might have overreacted just a little with the whole "calling fire down from heaven" thing. Is it just me or do you also feel for the first two groups a little bit? I mean, what had happened that would warrant such a response from God's rugged prophet? The back story can be found in 2 Kings 1:

"Now Ahaziah fell through the lattice of his

> *upper room in Samaria, and was injured; so he sent messengers and said to them, 'Go, inquire of Baal-Zebub, the god of Ekron, whether I shall recover from this injury.' But the angel of the LORD said to Elijah the Tishbite, 'Arise, go up to meet the messengers of the king of Samaria, and say to them, "Is it because there is no God in Israel that you are going to inquire of Baal-Zebub, the god of Ekron?" Now therefore, thus says the LORD: 'You shall not come down from the bed to which you have gone up, but you shall surely die.'" So Elijah departed." (2 Kings 1:2-4)*

That is why Elijah responded so harshly, furthering his feud with the family of Ahab. King Ahaziah was leading Israel in looking for answers everywhere except from the Lord. Sadly, we still do the same thing today. If the modern American Church were to identify with anyone in this story, she would most certainly identify with Ahaziah. Like the king, we have fallen, we are wounded, and we're seeking answers from everyone but God.

TUNE OUT THE NOISE

When we respond to the problems we are facing by seeking solutions from anything outside of God's Kingdom, we are bound for trouble. Haven't we seen this in the Church in recent years? Rather than increasingly becoming more like Jesus, we have become more and more like the world. Rather than our citizenship of Heaven becoming more and more apparent, we have adapted pretty well to the corrupt culture around us. How could this have ever happened to God's people? We made the exact same mistake Ahaziah made when we fell. We didn't seek the Lord.

There is only one way for a fallen Church to rise again. Heeding the voices that say the secret is to be trendier won't get us very far. The key is not found in adopting some seeker-sensitive model. Jesus said, *"My sheep hear My voice, and I know them, and they follow Me."* (John 10:27) As a matter of fact, before He made this statement, He said that those who truly belong to Him, *"Will by no means follow a stranger, but will flee from him, for they do not know the voice of strangers."* (John 10:5) The one way for the Church to rise up from this bed of affliction is by hearing and heeding the voice of God.

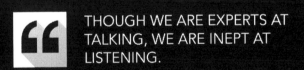

THOUGH WE ARE EXPERTS AT TALKING, WE ARE INEPT AT LISTENING.

The great challenge we now face is that though we are experts at talking, we are inept at listening. We have become so self-infatuated that we no longer seek the will of the Lord. We merely make up our minds and ask Him to bless our decision. A.W. Tozer hit the nail on the head when he said, "Most Christians don't hear God's voice because we've already decided we aren't going to do what He says."[1] The only way for the Church to get out of this rut is to tune out the noise, seek the voice of our Shepherd, and follow His instruction.

LOST BUT LISTENING

I am probably the world's worst when it comes to buying gifts for Christmas. Nothing pulls the spirit of procrastination out of me like holiday shopping. Every single year I miscalculate how much time I have left to make my rounds and end up waiting until the very last minute to purchase gifts. When time starts really ticking I sit myself down for a little pep talk where I commit to starting earlier and making smarter decisions next year so that I don't run out of time again. Nevertheless, I continue finding myself right back in the same predicament every year. It's as though I lose control and just step aboard the same ole sinking ship every holiday season. This past year was no exception.

One day while I was out going through all the picked-over stores pleading with God to help me find a suitable gift for my loved ones, I had an experience I'll never forget. A little boy, who was perhaps a year older than my son Judah, was running around the department store exploring every nook and cranny. I saw that familiar look in his eyes that I have seen in my son's eyes countless times, the look of awe and wonder. He was finding inspiration in the smallest things. No matter where the spirit of wonder led this little guy, I noticed that his dad's eyes were always on him. Still, however, at one point while they were in the men's clothing section he managed to slip out of sight. The dad's face said it all. Not having eyes on his son, he began to panic. He called out, "Jamie, Jamie, where are you?" I was a few aisles away from the dad, in the pants section, when suddenly I heard a little muffled voice respond, "Dad, I'm right here! Where are you? I can't see you!" Suddenly all panic melted away from this young father's face and he said, "I'm right here buddy." Jamie, the little boy, replied, "Where? I can't see you!" He had crawled in between a few clothing racks and couldn't seem to find his way out. The dad reassured his son that everything was alright, and he said, "Follow my voice." A few moments later there was Jamie, crawling out from behind some clothes, running straight to his father.

COME OUT OF HIDING

I believe right now God is speaking to His children saying, "Follow My voice." The Church is lost. Like Ahaziah, we've fallen, we're broken, and we can't seem to get out of the mess that we are in. We've looked in a million different directions. Nevertheless, if we will refuse to take another step down the path which Ahaziah chose, there is still hope. Things can still turn around. However, it all hinges on whether or not we will heed to the voice of the Lord. Heaven is calling us. Will you join the remnant that is following God's voice out of the wilderness we have been in?

We have no other option. Our world desperately needs the Church to come out of hiding. God will not use our voice until we heed His voice. In an Ahaziah culture God still has an Elijah company that will fearlessly trumpet the Word of the Lord. Before Christ returns, a people who know His voice and follow Him without reservation will take the stage. God is looking for those who have died to their agenda and have been made alive to the mandate of Heaven. Friend, it's time to follow the voice of Heaven and come out of hiding.

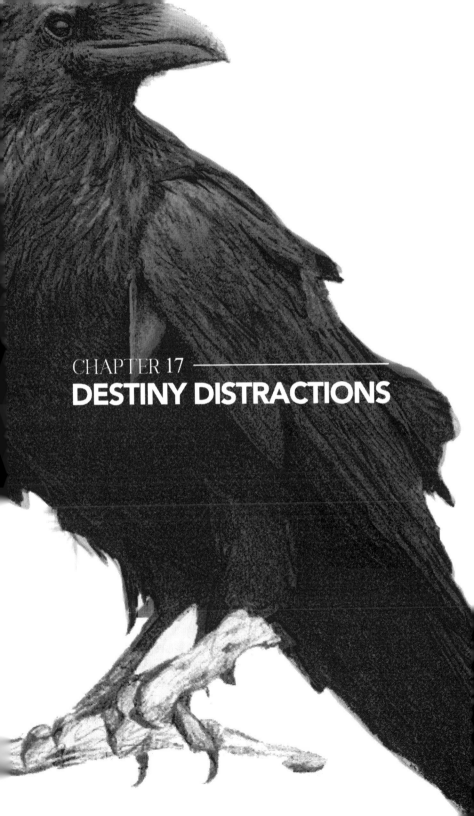

CHAPTER 17
DESTINY DISTRACTIONS

With the busy lives we live, if you have made it to this part of the book chances are there is something stirring deep inside of you. You know that you were strategically placed in the earth by God for this specific moment in time. You realize you have been called by the King Himself, and there is a remnant, handpicked by Heaven, that is destined to catch the flame of holy conviction and burn so brightly that those bound in darkness will come running to the light of Christ.

Nevertheless, the sad reality is that not all who have been called to this assignment end up playing the part for which they have been called. After all, it was Jesus that said in Matthew 22:14, *"Many are called, but few are chosen."* Why are few chosen? So few are chosen because so few are willing to pay the price. Please don't misunderstand me. Anytime a preacher begins talking about there being a price that we must pay someone immediately cries, "Legalism! Works!" To be clear, I am not talking about paying the price for salvation. We could never pay that price. Only Jesus, in His unmatched love, had the power to purchase our redemption. What I am talking about is what it will cost you to walk in your destiny.

Elisha quickly discovered this principle when he was being groomed as Elijah's successor. 2 Kings 2 begins by telling us that the hour of Elijah's departure had come. As Elisha was following him from a place called

Gilgal, Elijah turned and said to his protégé, *"'Stay here, please, for the LORD has sent me on to Bethel.' But Elisha said, 'As the LORD lives, and as your soul lives, I will not leave you!' So they went down to Bethel."* (2 Kings 2:2)

As they traveled on, some prophets from Bethel came to Elisha and told him that God was going to take Elijah from him that very day. Elisha paid their words of caution no mind, saying to them, *"Yes, I know; keep silent!"* (2 Kings 2:3)

Then Elijah turned to him again and told Elisha to stay there as he journeyed onto Jericho. Yet, Elisha persisted and went on with Elijah. As if the prophets from Bethel were not enough, more prophets came to Elisha from Jericho with the same message saying Elijah would soon be gone. Yet again Elisha paid them no mind and told them to keep silent.

You won't believe where the story goes next. It is totally unexpected — not! Elijah turned to Elisha a third time and said, *"Stay here, please, for the LORD has sent me on to the Jordan."* However, Elisha wasn't budging and again said, *"As the LORD lives, and as your soul lives, I will not leave you!"* (2 Kings 2:6)

Elisha must have felt like he was having a bad case of déjà vu. Sure enough, on the heels of him pledging his commitment to Elijah, he again saw the prophets coming in the distance just as they had done the first two times. Yet, this time when the prophets drew near, they did not come to tell him that Elijah would soon be taken away. This time they simply came to watch the event transpire in real-time.

The school of prophets watched as Elijah took his mantle and struck the Jordan river, causing the waters to supernaturally part so he and Elisha could cross over on dry ground. Then comes the climactic moment of this entire saga. The Bible says that Elijah said to Elisha,

> *"'Ask what may I do for you, before I am taken away from you?' Elisha said, 'Please let a double portion of your spirit be upon me.' So he said, 'You have asked a hard thing. Nevertheless, if you see me when I am taken from you, it shall be so for you; but if not, it shall not be so.' Then it happened, as they continued on and talked, that suddenly a chariot of fire appeared with horses of fire and separated the two of them; and Elijah went up by a whirlwind into heaven. And Elisha saw it." (2 Kings 2:9-12)*

DELIBERATE FOCUS

Did you catch that? Elisha had the audacity to ask for a double portion of the spirit that Elijah had walked in. Elijah made it clear to his protégé that what he was asking for was no small thing. Yet, the seasoned prophet told him plain and simple what it would cost for him to receive that which he was requesting. He simply told Elisha that if he saw him as he was being taken away, his request would be granted. In other words, Elijah was telling him that if he could just keep his focus, in spite of the chariots of fire and the whirlwind, he would have what he asked for. Verse twelve contains three little words that were the secret to the up-and-coming prophet's success. That verse begins by saying, "Elisha saw it..."

 THE CLOSER YOU GET TO YOUR DESTINY, THE MORE PREVALENT DISTRACTIONS BECOME.

What was the price Elisha had to pay to step into his destiny? It is the exact same price you and I will have to pay to step into ours — he had to fight to keep his focus. Had he been distracted by the school of prophets, the chariots of fire, or the whirlwind, he might not have caught a double portion. The weapon of distraction has been far more deadly among those who are called to stand under the mantle of Elijah in this hour than we have realized. Though many are called, few are chosen because they are preoccupied and miss their moment of opportunity. Your destiny to be one who will stand as a voice of truth in a corrupt culture hinges upon your deliberate focus. Do you have eyes that are fixed solely on Christ or do your eyes still wander from distraction to distraction? The closer you get to your destiny, the more prevalent distractions become. Dead men must be willing to pay the price of deliberate focus.

DRIVING UP ON DISTRACTIONS

I live in one of America's vacation hotspots. With over 12 million visitors annually, we get to meet a vast array of people from many different places.[1] As a native of the region surrounding the Great Smoky Mountains, I must admit that until my late teens I did not see what others found so fascinating about vacationing here. In recent years my appreciation for the beauty of my hometown has grown immensely, but still I am a beach guy when it comes to vacation. Though our mountains are truly breathtaking, I would prefer to be surrounded by a sandy beach and saltwater any day.

You might think I have a pretty bad case of beach-fever, but my wife takes it to a whole new level! Part of why I love going to the coast so much is because of how much Ali loves it. Every summer I can almost guarantee we will end up beaching it at some point or another. It is one of the biggest highlights of our year. Whenever our vacation comes to a close and we start the stretch back home, we do so already discussing when we will get to go back. I could tell you countless memories that we've made along the way.

There's just something about overpacking our suitcases at the last minute, cramming them into the vehicle, and then driving twelve hours to the beach that makes Ali and I feel like kids on Christmas morning. We love it! A few years ago on our trip I noticed something that I had not acknowledged prior to that vacation. Once we left our house and got out of our town, we did not see one souvenir shop for the entire twelve-hour drive. Not one. Yet, when we got off of the exit, which was about 30 minutes from the condo we were renting, these little tourist shops started popping up everywhere. You know the kind of shops I'm talking about, those where you can go and buy a turtle shaped magnet with the name of the beach on it for the special price of only $19.99. What a deal! Here is what I noticed, and it has remained true every time since. The closer we got to the beach, the more those shops kept popping up. Finally, upon reaching the main strip, these little shops were as far as the eye could see. And, lucky for me, my family wanted to check each one of them out so they could get their special magnet.

At one point I checked my phone and saw that we were within five minutes of the place we were staying. Guess what? Nearly three hours later we were finally pulling in to start unpacking. Do you know why? Because the closer we got to our destination, the more distractions we had to deal with.

YOU'RE GETTING CLOSE

How have distractions been in your life lately? If you feel like the enemy has been vying for your attention at every turn it could be a sign that you are stepping into your destiny. I want to encourage you to fix your eyes on Jesus and keep pressing toward the assignment He is calling you to. There are some defining moments coming in the days ahead for those who will say yes to the Elijah mandate. Hell would love nothing more than to have you distracted so that you fail to seize the moment.

Elisha was destined for the day he was stepping into. Nevertheless, everything hinged on whether or not he would ignore the distractions and remain focused. By God's grace, you don't have to live at the mercy of whatever distractions come your way. You can lock your eyes on Jesus and raise your voice, until awakening shakes this generation. You were born for this moment!

CHAPTER 18
RUDE AWAKENING

Ali and I had the scare of our lives as a young married couple on the day that we moved into our first home. Let me explain. We were so excited to finally be getting our own place. We had looked far and wide, feeling hopeless at times. Then, we found our "perfect" first home! It wasn't anything fancy, but it was ours. We were ecstatic! While we patiently awaited closing day, we began torturing ourselves almost every night by binge watching home renovation shows and dreaming of what we could do after all the papers were signed and the place was officially ours. We scraped together enough money for a fresh coat of paint, new floors, and some decorative pieces.

Once we closed and they gave us the keys, we took about two weeks before we moved in and got to work! When I say "we" got to work, I mean that Ali's dad got to work. He listened to our vision for the house and while we were in and out of town, out of the goodness of his heart, he did absolutely everything for us. We were blown away by his generosity, and by how well everything turned out.

The process of owning our own place quickly revealed that I had a lot to learn. As a young, naive, first-time homeowner I was in for a rude awakening when we finally moved in, quite literally. You see, while all of my attention was directed towards the aesthetics, it never even crossed my mind that I also needed to look into some

RUDE AWAKENING

of the more pertinent, yet often overlooked, issues like the home's air filter, or replacing burned out light bulbs, or what I would soon be directing all of my attention toward — the fire alarm system.

After a long hard day of moving all of our belongings into the house, Ali and I were finally headed to bed, cuddled up on a mattress on the floor. I'll never forget that night. It had started storming outside. The sound of the heavy rain pelting the ground on the other side of our window made for a cozy night of deep sleep. While we were both out like a rock, at about three in the morning, our fire alarm began blaring, and I do mean blaring! We both jolted out of bed in a panic. Could our newly renovated home be burning to the ground? I ran from one end of the house to the other looking for fire and smelling for smoke, but there was nothing. Once assured there was no fire, I started pushing on each smoke detector until they finally quit squealing.

The next day we had someone come out to check everything. He could not determine what had tripped the alarm. After testing our system he told us we had nothing to worry about; it was an apparent fluke. A few months passed and again, in the middle of the night, the same thing happened. I got up and started running through the house looking for what had set off the alarm. Again, nothing. So, we called for a second opinion, and they too came to the same conclusion as the first guy.

Sadly, every few months we would wake up from a dead sleep to the same old screeching sound ringing through our home. Beyond the fact that the professionals had assured me the smoke detectors were fine, I knew first-hand they were working because Ali and I would try to cook at least once a week! We are not called to be chefs by any stretch of the imagination.

Each time that they would go off in the middle of the night I would jump up out of bed and run around the house like a mad man looking for the problem until one day, after we had lived there for about a year, I did something different. It was about three in the morning and the alarm went off again. I was annoyed but I calmly wiped the sleep from my eyes and slowly walked through the house to ensure that everything was fine. My reaction had started to change. A few months later it went off again. At first, I put the pillow over my head. I waited about five minutes and then I finally got up and started looking around. Eventually, while I was searching for any sign of fire or smoke, the alarm turned off on its own, a first in my experience. A few months later when the alarm sounded, I stayed in bed. I looked over and saw that Ali and I had the same idea. We were just lying there, each covering our head with a pillow. Over the next several months that fire alarm would periodically go off and each time we would just take our pillows, put them over our heads, and ignore the alarm until it turned off. I never even got up to see if anything in the house was going on that I should be concerned with.

Finally, one night when it was going off yet again, it hit me. After we laid there for about ten minutes, I knew we were in trouble. There wasn't a fire or anything to be concerned with. That wasn't the troubling issue. As I looked over to see Ali sleeping through the noise as we both again covered our heads, what hit me was the reality that the alarm no longer alarmed us. We had come to a place where we simply tuned out that which should have provoked a sense of urgency within us.

SLEEPING THROUGH THE ALARM

Friend, this book was written to draw attention to the fact that America is sleeping through the alarm. What once alarmed us no longer concerns us. You know a society is in trouble when their people no longer care about sin. You know the Church is in trouble when God's people no longer care about compromise. Ignorance, much less willful ignorance, is not bliss. We cannot turn a blind eye to babies being murdered in the womb, children being forced into sex trafficking, the rise of racism and violence, or any other abomination we have tolerated in this nation. As grim as the future of our country might seem when considering the reality of such blatant sin and compromise, I see a light rising that will vanquish the darkness. Who will carry this light into our world? Only those who have died to self and are alive to Christ. Heaven is calling for dead men to stand up—Heaven is calling your name! Will you give your life for this cause?

Elisha's response to Heaven's beckoning gives a strategic framework for how we should respond to God's plan for our lives. As a fiery horse-drawn chariot raced by Elijah and Elisha, separating them from one another, Elisha diligently kept his focus in the right direction as he watched his leader get carried to Heaven by a whirlwind. Although Elisha knew this moment was coming, his heart was filled with anguish. The Bible captures Elisha's vulnerable response to seeing Elijah whisked away by saying, *"And Elisha saw it, and he cried out, 'My father, my father, the chariot of Israel and its horsemen!' So he saw him no more. And he took hold of his own clothes and tore them into two pieces." (2 Kings 2:12)* In spite of the undeniable pain Elisha was feeling, he yet continued to keep his focus. This passage goes on to say, *"He also took up the mantle of Elijah that had fallen from him." (2 Kings 2:13)*

PICK IT UP

In the closing of this book may I ask, who is going to pick up this mantle? Thank God for all the great revivalists in our past. In studying their lives I am overwhelmed by the courage that so many men and women chose to embrace as they stood against the evil tide of their day. Yet, I must say, with no disrespect to them or the heroic lives they lived, their day has long passed. I am thankful for John Wesley and George

Whitfield, but their day has passed. Thank God for Jonathan Edwards and Charles Finney but their day has passed. Thank God for William Seymour but his day has passed. I could go on and on mentioning the lives of men and women who were strategic in taking a stand for holiness and righteousness in their day, but the real question is, who will do it in our day? The mantles once carried by these mighty men and women have been dropped and Heaven is watching to see if there are any who are willing to lay down their lives to pick them up and prepare the way for the return of Christ.

I know there is hope because God has left you in the earth. I believe there is a remnant ready to stand up to the injustice taking place in our nation just as Elijah stood up to the injustice taking place in Israel. God is not calling us to do as so many have wrongfully done in the past and follow Elijah as a model. Rather He is calling us to follow the mandate Elijah walked in and stand up as a voice of reckoning. America is ripe for another awakening. If we will give our lives for the cause of Heaven's Kingdom nothing can stop us from reaching this generation. Hell is convinced that the fate of this generation is sealed and they will spend eternity separated from God. Yet, Heaven has another plan. If we will deny ourselves, take up our cross, and follow after Christ, we *will* see the tide turn. It is time for dead men to arise!

SOURCES

Chapter 1
1. Disturb us, Lord | https://renovare.org/articles/disturb-us-lord

Chapter 2
1. Deitrich Bonhoeffer, The Cost of Discipleship | https://www.goodreads.com/quotes/98256-when-christ-calls-a-man-he-bids-him-come-and

Chapter 6
1. John Wesley quote | https://www.azquotes.com/quote/311549?ref=fear-nothing
2. Definition - Cherith root word: Strong's'#H3772
3. Ravens are thieves | https://news.softpedia.com/news/10-Amazing-Facts-About-Ravens-70914.shtml

Chapter 7
1. https://www.nationalgeographic.com/animals/article/year-of-the-bird-brains-intelligence-smarts
2. https://www.mentalfloss.com/article/53295/10-fascinating-facts-about-ravens
3. https://www.azquotes.com/quote/1339969

Chapter 9
1. https://www.thebrandingjournal.com/2015/05/what-to-learn-from-tropicanas-packaging-redesign-failure/

Chapter 10
1. https://biblehub.com/hebrew/6886.htm

Chapter 11
1. http://www.fathers.com/statistics-and-research/the-extent-of-fatherlessness/
2. https://thefatherlessgeneration.wordpress.com/statistics/

Chapter 12
1. https://www.gospeltruth.net/1868_75Independent/731204_conscience.htm

Chapter 13
1. https://www.telegraph.co.uk/books/authors/35-great-quotes-about-scotland-and-the-scots/35-great- quotes-about-scotland-and-the-scots11/

Chapter 16
1. https://www.azquotes.com/quote/1137461

Chapter 17
1. https://www.visitmysmokies.com/blog/smoky-mountains/great-smoky-mountains-national-park-visitors-record/

ABOUT THE AUTHOR

CALEB PIERCE is a husband, father, speaker, and author who has a passion to see the Church revived and the world awakened. He and his wife Ali live in Knoxville, Tennessee with their one son, Judah. They are honored to serve in leadership at The Lift Church, led by Pastors Keith and Margie Nix. In 2017, Caleb and Ali released their first book, *The Rules Of Romance Before Marriage: Answers To The Top 50 Questions The Unmarried Are Asking About Dating, Sex and Purity.* Then in 2019 Caleb released his second book, *Jesus Isn't A Hipster.*

CALEBPIERCE.ORG | THELIFTCHURCH.TV

MORE FROM
THE LIFT PUBLISHING GROUP

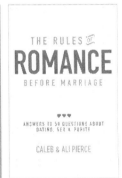

THELIFTSTORE.ORG

Made in the USA
Middletown, DE
01 November 2022

13870931R00106